SCOTLAND AND THE IMPACT OF THE GREAT WAR 1914–1928

SCOTLAND AND THE IMPACT OF THE GREAT WAR 1914–1928

John A. Kerr

HODDER
GIBSON
AN HACHETTE UK COMPANY

The front cover shows the lych gate in front of Fogo Kirkyard near Duns in the Scottish Borders. The lych gate was built as a memorial to soldiers killed in the First World War and the names of the war dead can be seen at the entrance to the Kirkyard. The insert image shows the Machine Gun Section of the 3rd Gordon Highlanders in 1915.

Dedication
Nettlehill

The Publishers would like to thank the following for permission to reproduce copyright material:

Photo credits Source 1.2 Hulton Archive/Getty Images; Source 1.3 © Fine Art Photographic Library/CORBIS; Source 1.4 Courtesy of The Scottish Mining Museum Trust; Source 1.5 Reproduced with the permission of Glasgow City Council, Glasgow Museums; Source 1.6 Eyemouth Museum Trust/Scran; Source 1.7 © World History Archive/Alamy; Source 1.8 Hulton Archive/Getty Images; Source 1.9 Hulton Archive/Getty Images; Source 1.10 Mary Evans Picture Library; Source 1.11 © Mary Evans Picture Library/Alamy; Source 1.12 © TopFoto/ Houghton; Source 2.1 Reproduced by permission of the Trustees of the National Library of Scotland; Source 2.2 © Bettmann/CORBIS; Source 2.3 © Mary Evans Picture Library/Alamy; Source 2.4 FPG/Hulton Archive/Getty Images; Source 2.5 John Kerr; Source 2.6 © Pictorial Press Ltd/Alamy; Source 2.7 ©Dumfries and Galloway Council. Licensor www.scran.ac.uk; Source 2.8 Heart of Midlothian FC; Source 2.12 Mary Evans Picture Library; Source 2.13 World History Archive/TopFoto; Source 2.14 © INTERFOTO/Alamy; Source 2.15 © 2008 Lightroom Photos/TopFoto; Source 3.1 © Hulton-Deutsch Collection/CORBIS; Source 3.2 Australian History Museum, Macquarie University; Source 3.3 © Hulton-Deutsch Collection/CORBIS; Source 3.4 Dundee Central Library/Scran; Source 3.5 Reproduced by permission of the Trustees of the National Library of Scotland; Source 3.6 © Mary Evans Picture Library/Alamy; Source 3.7 Springburn Museum Trust/Scran; Source 3.8 Herald and Times Group; Source 3.9 Gallacher Memorial Library – Glasgow Caledonian University Library/Scran; Source 3.10 Reproduced with the permission of Glasgow City Council, Glasgow Museums; Source 3.11 ©Punch Limited/Topham; Source 3.12 © Dave and Sigrun Tollerton/Alamy; Source 3.13 John Kerr; Source 3.14 Courtesy of The Scots at War Trust; Source 3.15 Robert James; Source 4.1 topfoto.co.uk; Source 4.3 © Peter Nisbett. Licensor www.scran.ac.uk; Source 4.4 ©Scottish Life Archive, National Museums of Scotland. Licensor www.scran.ac.uk; Source 4.5 Mary Evans Picture Library/ONSLOW AUCTIONS LIMITED; Source 4.6 © CORBIS; Source 4.7 www.topfoto.co.uk; Source 4.8 Topical Press Agency/Hulton Archive/Getty Images; Source 4.9 Print Collector/HIP/TopFoto; Source 4.10 Topical Press Agency/Getty Images; Source 4.11 © Hulton-Deutsch Collection/CORBIS; Source 5.1 Hulton Archive/Getty Images; Source 5.2 National Museums Scotland/Scran; Source 5.3 www.topfoto. co.uk; Source 5.4 Glasgow Museums/Scran; Source 5.5 Gallacher Memorial Library – Glasgow Caledonian University Library/Scran; Source 5.6 Gallacher Memorial Library/Scran; Source 5.7 Reproduced with the permission of Glasgow City Council, Glasgow Museums; Source 5.8 ©RIA Novosti/TopFoto; Source 5.9 W.D. Kerr Collection/Scran; Source 6.1 © Illustrated London News Ltd/Mary Evans; Source 6.2 Mainstream Publishing.

Every effort has been made to trace all copyright holders, but if any have been inadvertently overlooked the Publishers will be pleased to make the necessary arrangements at the first opportunity.

Although every effort has been made to ensure that website addresses are correct at time of going to press, Hodder Gibson cannot be held responsible for the content of any website mentioned in this book. It is sometimes possible to find a relocated web page by typing in the address of the home page for a website in the URL window of your browser.

Hachette's policy is to use papers that are natural, renewable and recyclable products and made from wood grown in sustainable forests. The logging and manufacturing processes are expected to conform to the environmental regulations of the country of origin.

Orders: please contact Bookpoint Ltd, 130 Milton Park, Abingdon, Oxon OX14 4SB. Telephone: (44) 01235 827720. Fax: (44) 01235 400454. Lines are open 9.00–5.00, Monday to Saturday, with a 24-hour message answering service. Visit our website at www.hoddereducation.co.uk. Hodder Gibson can be contacted direct on: Tel: 0141 848 1609; Fax: 0141 889 6315; email: hoddergibson@hodder.co.uk

© John A. Kerr 2010
First published in 2010 by
Hodder Gibson, an imprint of Hodder Education,
An Hachette UK Company,
2a Christie Street
Paisley PA1 1NB

Impression number   5 4
Year   2013 2012

Cover photo © Robert James; The Gordon Highlanders Museum (insert)
Illustrations by Jeff Edwards
Typeset in Typeset in Sabon 10pt by Pantek Media
Printed in Dubai

A catalogue record for this title is available from the British Library
ISBN: 978 0340 987 551

Contents

Introduction

Who is this book for?

The books in this series are for students following the new Scottish Higher History Course. Each book in this series covers all you need to know about one of the most popular topics in Paper 2 of the newly revised Scottish Higher History course. The entire syllabus is covered so you can be sure all your needs will be met.

What is in this book?

This book is about Scotland and the Imapct of the Great War 1914–1928. From 2011, Paper 2 of your Higher History exam is completely different from any earlier Higher History exam paper. There are five completely new Scottish-based topics. These topics are:

- The Wars of Independence 1286–1328

- The Age of the Reformation 1542–1603

- The Treaty of Union 1689–1740

- Migration and Empire 1830–1939

- The Impact of the Great War 1914–1928

Each topic is divided into six sections. Check out the Arrangements document on the SQA website at: www.sqa.org.uk. There you will find detailed descriptions of the content that is in each and every topic in Paper 2.

The first section you will see is called 'Background'. The last section is called 'Perspective'. Neither of those sections will have any questions asked about them. They are NOT examined. That leaves four main issues, and each one of those issues has a question linked to it.

Topic: The impact of the Great War 1914–1928	
Background	looks at the political, social and economic conditions in Scotland on the eve of the Great War.
Issue 1	considers voluntary recruitment and the experience of Scottish soldiers on the Western Front and their contribution to the war effort.
Issue 2	looks at recruitment and conscription, and the reasons why some men did not want to fight. It considers the changing role of women during the war and the effect of the loss of Scottish soldiers on society.
Issue 3	considers the effect of the war on Scottish industry, agriculture and fishing and explores the knock-on effects on everyday life. It also looks at issues of emigration after the war.
Issue 4	looks at the political impact of the war and the crisis of Scottish identity.
Perspective	considers the role that the Great War played in the development of Scottish identity.

What do I have to do to be successful?

In Paper 2, all assessments will be in the form of questions based on primary or secondary sources and in this book there is full coverage of all four types of questions you will meet. You will have five sources to use and four questions to answer.

You will have 1 hour and 25 minutes to do that. That means you will have about 20 minutes to deal with each question so your answers must be well structured and well developed. Put simply, that means you must do three things in each question:

1 You must do what you are asked to do.

2 You must refer to information in the source.

3 You must also include your own relevant recalled knowledge.

In the final chapter of this book there are not only examples of questions, but also full explanations of what makes good and not so good answers to the differing questions. Each type of question has its own particular process you must use to answer it successfully. In this section you will also find clear explanations of how marks are allocated so that your answers can be structured to gain the best possible score.

What types of questions will I be asked?

There are FOUR different types of question. Each type will be in your exam paper.

Question Type 1 is a source evaluation question worth 5 marks. It will usually be identified with a question asking, 'How useful is Source A as evidence…'

In this type of question you are being asked to judge how good the source is as a piece of historical evidence.

Question Type 2 is a comparison question worth 5 marks. You will be asked to compare two points of view overall and in detail. The question MIGHT NOT use the word 'compare' in the question.

The wording of the question could be something like 'To what extent does Source B agree with Source C about...'

Question Type 3 is a 'How far' question and is worth 10 marks. This question is to test your knowledge on one specific part of an issue, called a sub-issue. You can find all the sub-issues in the column called 'detailed descriptors' on the SQA syllabus website at: www.sqa.org.uk.

Question Type 4 is a 'How fully' question and is worth 10 marks. This question is to test your knowledge of a whole issue. Remember there are four issues in the syllabus on which you can be examined.

To summarise...

This book will help you to be successful in Paper 2 of the Scottish Higher History course. To be successful you must recognise the type of question you are being asked, follow the process for answering that type of question and also show off your own knowledge of the topic.

Beware: The four question types explained here WILL appear in the exam paper every year but will NOT appear in the same order every year. You will need to stay alert and be ready for them in any order.

Scotland in 1914

Source 1.1

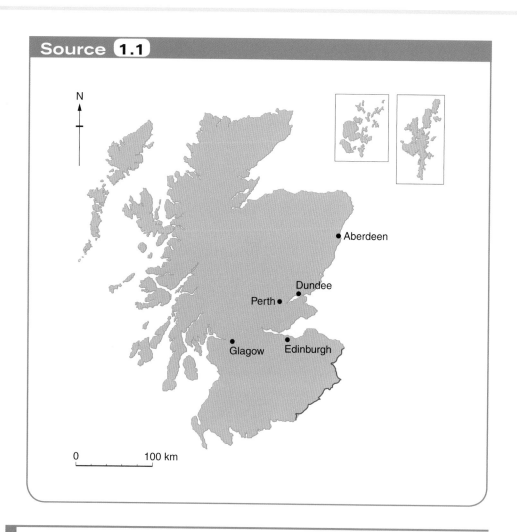

Scotland on the eve of the Great War

In 1900 Scotland had a population of about 4.5 million – not much different from today. Like today, most of the population lived in or near the four main cities – Glasgow, Edinburgh, Dundee and Aberdeen. Scotland was becoming an urbanised society. Urbanisation means the growth of towns and cities as people move from the countryside into the towns, usually in search of work and a better life. In 1850, one Scot in five lived in Glasgow, Edinburgh, Dundee or Aberdeen. By 1900, it was one in every three.

Scottish cities faced a huge overcrowding problem. The 1901 census showed almost 70 per cent of people in Glasgow lived in one- or two-roomed houses and 90 per cent of those people shared a toilet with another family. In Edinburgh and Leith 50 per cent of the people lived in one- or two-roomed houses and even in Perth the figure was 41 per cent. Visitors to

Victorian Scotland marvelled at the country's growing wealth but were appalled by living conditions in the cities where, according to one visitor, cleanliness was preserved in bug-infested houses with one cold-water tap in a kitchen sink.

Source 1.2

Edinburgh around 1900. Britain had not been involved in a major war for almost 100 years. Within the next 20 years the lives of all the people in this photo and in Scotland would be affected in some way by the Great War.

Migration from the countryside was one of the main reasons for the growth of cities. By 1900 the population of rural areas from the Highlands to the Borders was falling and the number of people who worked in farming had fallen to 11 per cent of the working population.

Between 1904 and 1913 over half a million people left Scotland, mostly for the USA, Canada and Australasia. Not all emigrants were successful. About one in three of all Scots emigrants eventually returned home. Irish migration to Scotland was still an important factor in Scotland's population before 1914, especially in west central Scotland. The Catholic population of Glasgow increased by 100,000 between 1875 and 1900. Immigrants also came from Italy and Lithuania in large numbers around 1900.

The nineteenth century had seen big changes in the Highlands. Arguments still rage about the cause of these changes. Some argue that the Highland way of life could not continue – a growing population trying to survive on scarce resources was one reason for change. Some believe that change was forced on the Highlands by landowners trying to increase their income from their land, while others blame the growth of a tourist industry that wanted empty spaces with ruined houses, romantic castles, deer on the hills, grouse on the moors and, in the evening, highland dancing and bagpipes playing. In a word, tourists wanted 'Balmoralism', so called after Queen Victoria's highland estate.

Source 1.3

'Balmoralism' or 'Highlandism' encouraged a shortbread-tin stereotype of Scotland. In that world the Highlands were lonely, empty places. For Highland Scots the choice was often poverty or migration but tourists did not want to see the reality.

Whatever side of the argument is supported, the fact remains that Highlanders moved out of the Highlands either to lowland cities or abroad to Canada, New Zealand and other parts of the Empire. For those who stayed, life was hard with many Highlanders living on poor strips of land near the coast. These crofters became angry and that anger erupted in the

early 1880s. The government was startled by the violent protests of the crofters on Lewis and Skye and appointed Lord Napier to investigate their grievances. His report stated that Highlanders lived in a state of misery and spoke of patient long suffering without parallel in the history of our country. Mainly as a result of this report, public opinion turned in favour of the Highlanders and led to the Crofter's Act of 1886 which stopped forced evictions and ended the right of landowners to charge whatever they wanted for rent. But the 'land question' in the Highlands remained unresolved.

The Scottish economy in 1914

Before 1914 the Central Belt of Scotland was a powerhouse for shipbuilding, engineering and the production of coal, iron and steel. Glasgow was known as 'the second city of the Empire'. Scotland – certainly in the Central Belt – was booming. The introduction to Edwin Muir's *Scottish Journey*, written in the early 1930s, reported:

> *The Clyde in 1913 launched 750,000 tons of shipping, more than the total output of either Germany or the USA, and equivalent to 18 per cent of world production. Scotland manufactured about a fifth of the UK's steel output and 13.5 per cent of its pig iron. It employed 150,000 coal-miners. In textiles, the jute industry of Dundee and the tweed mills of the Borders were in the full flood of prosperity.*

T.C. Smout (Introduction), in Edwin Muir, Scottish Journey, 1996 (first published 1935)

International trade was vital to the Scottish economy. The economy relied on overseas markets and even in agriculture, international trade was vital. Britain was nowhere near self-sufficient in food. In any one week home-produced food could only feed the Scottish population for the equivalent of two days. For the other five days food had to come from abroad.

Another worrying development was foreign competition and some Scottish factory owners even started building factories abroad (such as Jute factories in Calcutta) to take advantage of lower wage costs. This created more competition for Scottish exports – but kept the private profits of the owners high! Meanwhile, many Scottish owners did not want to spend their profits on new technology and this resulted in even greater competition for Scotland in the global marketplace.

Globalisation, trade and the Scottish economy

Globalisation is a modern word but the idea of globalisation can be applied to the British Empire at the end of the nineteenth century. As a result of international trade, financial investment, migration of people and the spread of technology, the Scottish economy reached out across the world.

Bruce Lenman illustrates some aspects of this global involvement. He wrote:

 The wheat of the Canadian or American prairies had to be taken by rail to eastern ports. The locomotive could well be made in Glasgow while the sacks holding the grain were quite likely to have been manufactured in Dundee. The ships that carried the grain across the North Atlantic were probably built on the Clyde.

Quoted in Tom Devine, The Scottish Nation 1700–2007, 2006, page 255

Lenman makes the point that while the food eaten in Scotland (in this case wheat) was grown abroad, the transportation involved in getting it to Scotland was the result of Scottish manufacturers and British investment abroad. Even the sacks that held the wheat existed only because of the part played by Dundee in the international economy. (See section on textiles.)

As already mentioned, international trade was vital to the Scottish economy. Thirty eight per cent of all Scottish coal mined was exported. From Border knitwear to whisky to herring – all of these industries depended on the international market. If trade was disrupted or export markets lost, Scotland's economy would face problems – but to most people, and the tens of thousands employed, Scotland's economy looked in good shape before 1914.

Coal

Between 1880 and 1914 coal was Scotland's fastest growing industry and in 1900 more than 150,000 miners worked in Scotland's coalmines. The coal seams in the west of Scotland were dying out while the fastest growth was in Fife and Lothian. Leith, Grangemouth and Methil exported across the North Sea to Eastern Europe and Russia. However, by 1914 even the coal industry was falling behind the times. New industries such as oil, gas production and electricity would soon cut demand for coal in people's homes. While foreign competition would take away markets, mine owners were slow to invest in new, more efficient technology and in 1913 four out of every five tonnes of coal taken from Scottish pits were still cut by miners using picks and shovels.

Source 1.4

Coal was THE power source in Scotland around 1900 and lack of investment in new technology ensured miner's lives remained hard and dangerous.

Iron and steel

By 1900 new technology had made possible the mass production of a new wonder metal – steel. Previously, Scotland had specialised in iron production but resources of iron ore were running out. Now demand for steel created boomtowns such as Airdrie, Coatbridge, Mossend and Wishaw. By 1911 Scottish steel towns were producing over one million tonnes each year. Steel is stronger than iron but is harder to work with and only one forge in Scotland was capable of producing quality steel. The Parkhead Forge in Glasgow, owned by William Beardmore, invested in huge steam hammers that could beat and shape the steel and, according to eyewitnesses, could make the whole area around Parkhead quiver 'as in an earthquake'. The company specialised in making armour plate for the Royal Navy's latest battleships – one example of how Scotland's heavy industries were interlinked. The naval race with Germany, in the build up to the war, provided a huge boost for these industries.

Shipbuilding

Shipbuilding depended heavily on international trade, carrying Scottish exports around the world. In 1879 the world's first ocean-going steel-hulled ship was launched on the Clyde and within a few years all shipyards had switched to building with steel. Orders from around the world flooded into the Clyde. When Beardmore's company opened their shipbuilding yard at Dalmuir in 1902 there were already 40 different yards on the Clyde.

Source 1.5

The staff of Bay 3 at William Beardmore and Company's Howitzer Department, Parkhead, during the First World War. A howitzer is a short gun for high-angle firing of shells. When the First World War broke out, Beardmore was one of the companies the British Government turned to for the manufacture of naval guns.

By 1914 almost 20 per cent of the world's shipping was built on the Clyde and although foreign competition had increased, the Clyde yards had one important source for orders – the Royal Navy. The building of HMS Dreadnought in 1905 started a naval race with Germany that secured the fortunes of the shipyards at least until the end of the war. But what would happen when the war ended?

Fishing

The spread of the railways allowed fresh fish to be transported across Britain and fishing ports began to prosper. By the 1880s trawling had become established in Aberdeen and these trawlers specialised in white fish such as cod and haddock. However, the main catch for Scotland's fleet of sailing boats was herring. Herring migrate in huge shoals around the coast of Britain and so the boats followed the fish as they moved. As the boats trawled the waters of Scotland and eastern England, fisherwomen would travel to the ports to gut the fish and pack them into barrels for export to Russia or Germany. Boat crews and fisherwomen from Eyemouth in the Borders travelled as far as Wick in the far north of Scotland and Yarmouth in eastern England – all following 'the shoals o' herring'. But what would happen when the export markets in Eastern Europe vanished?

Source 1.6

These Eyemouth fisher lassies travelled huge distances to support their men on the herring boats – but their livelihoods were also changed by the war.

Textiles

Although textile production was in decline by 1900, it was still a major employer.

Jute was a good example of an industry dependent on international trade. The raw material for sacking, jute, was grown in Bengal (now Bangladesh but then part of the British Empire). Jute was brought to Dundee and was softened by whale oil (Dundee was a famous whaling port) and used to make anything from coal sacks to nose bags for horses. During the war it was used to produce millions of sand bags. In Dundee over 70 jute mills employed tens of thousands of people, especially women. In the biggest factory, Camperdown, 14,000 people were employed. But 'Juteopolis', as Dundee was known, was already facing difficulties from foreign competition. Factories in India were being developed with Scottish technology and investment!

In Paisley, cotton was king and especially cotton thread – so much so that by 1896 J and P Coats controlled most of the world's thread industry. As in other textile towns, Paisley's factories provided work for tens of thousands of workers. Connected to the thread industry, the sewing machine industry also grew. In 1856 Isaac Singer opened a shop in Glasgow and by 1885 the Singer Sewing factory in Kilbowie, Clydebank, was Europe's biggest factory, making 10,000 sewing machines every week.

Source 1.7

The Camperdown jute factory employed over 14,000 people! What happened to them when the jute industry collapsed?

The Highlands

Although some industry was growing in the Highlands – whisky making, Harris Tweed and aluminium – there was no huge benefit to most of the Highland population. Distilleries employed few people. Whisky blending and storage took place mainly in the lowlands. Harris Tweed faced strong competition until the Harris Tweed Association was formed in 1909 to protect its homemade tweed. Despite this, changing fashions meant that the future of tweed was not guaranteed. Although Scotland produced one-third of the world's aluminium before the First World War, the building of factories at the Falls of Foyers and Kinlochleven had more to do with the availability of hydro-electricity than providing jobs or bringing prosperity to the Highlands.

Before – and after – the Great War the real issue in the Highlands was the 'Land Question'. Although the Crofters Act of 1886 provided a major improvement in rents, the removal of eviction threats and more secure occupation of crofts, the 'Land Question' would return to haunt politicians after the war. Before the war, emigration, usually to Canada, took Highlanders off in search of opportunity and secure land ownership. These patterns of emigration resumed when the war ended.

Summary

In 1914 the Scottish economy looked strong and healthy, especially when the arms race with Germany brought orders for more coal, steel, iron and ships. However, Scotland's heavy industries were all interlinked and each was dependant on the others' success. The Scottish economy faced serious, but so far hidden, structural weaknesses. By 1914 it was clear that the world was buying less from Scotland. If trade was disrupted and export markets were lost the Scottish economy would suffer. This was one of the causes of Scotland's difficulties after the Great War.

Scottish politics in 1914

The Liberals

The Liberals dominated Scottish politics before 1914. As Andrew Marr wrote in *The Battle for Scotland*, 'Through most of the Victorian period, Scotland had provided the Liberals with a loyal regiment of silent, dough-faced MPs.' (Marr, *The Battle for Scotland*, 1992) However, 30 years after the start of the war the Liberals had declined to a poor third behind the Conservative and Unionist Party and the Labour Party.

In 1914 the Liberal Party was the strongest political party in Scotland. The other parties – the Conservatives, the Labour Party and the Unionists – posed no real threat. In the election of 1910 the Liberals won 57 out of 70 Scottish seats. The Unionists and Conservatives won 10 seats between them and the Labour Party won 3 seats.

The Great War was a catalyst for Liberal decline but why were the Liberals so popular with voters before the war? Were the Liberals really so strong before 1914? Were the other political parties really so weak?

There were several reasons why so many voters supported the Liberals before the Great War. The Liberals seemed to challenge the power of the privileged aristocracy and big businessmen and to many working- and middle-class voters this was a vote winner!

The Liberals also benefited politically from their opposition to the big landowners. In the Highlands the 'land question' and the struggle of the crofting communities had gained widespread publicity. In fact an enquiry by the Labour Party in 1911 concluded, 'The Land Question in Scotland dominated everything else. Scotland has stood by the Liberal Government so solidly because it hates the House of Lords and the Landlords.'

Another reason for support was the rise of New Liberal ideas. Traditionally, Liberals had argued that they stood for the least possible government interference in the lives of ordinary people. However, by the end of the nineteenth century it was clear that poverty and social problems could not be solved by self-help alone. The New Liberals argued that state intervention was necessary to help people deal with social problems over which they had no control.

> ## Source 1.8
>
> **The Liberal Party was hugely popular in Scotland before 1914. This poster from just before the Great War gives some clues as to why.**
>
>
>
> THE DAWN OF HOPE.
>
> NATIONAL INSURANCE AGAINST SICKNESS AND DISABLEMENT
>
> Mr. LLOYD GEORGE'S National Health Insurance Bill provides for the insurance of the Worker in case of Sickness.
>
> **Support the Liberal Government**
> in their policy of
> **SOCIAL REFORM.**

The New Liberals argued that a minimum wage, old age pensions and unemployment and sickness benefits would all help the lives of the poor. They also promised to tackle the housing crisis in a similar way to the land question by weakening the power of landlords and improving the rights of occupiers. As a result, thousands of working class men who had been given the vote in 1867 and 1884 hoped for real improvement in their lives from the Liberal Party's commitment to social reform. Lord Tweedsmuir, better known as the novelist John Buchan, reported in 1911, 'Liberals alone understood and sympathised with the poor; a working man who was not a Liberal was inaccessible to reason.' (Quoted in Devine, *The Scottish Nation 1700–2007*, 2006) (Lord Tweedsmuir thought any working man would be utterly foolish not to support the Liberals – yet Tweedsmuir was a Conservative!)

The Liberals also gained energy from the 'Young Scots', an energetic and popular group within the Liberal Party that issued propaganda leaflets and took the Liberal message on to the streets. The Young Scots cleverly combined patriotism with social reform, arguing that a London-based parliament would never give enough time to discussing and reforming Scottish social problems. In towns and cities the Young Scots developed and publicised Liberal policies as an alternative to socialism. By 1910 the Young Scots society had 2500 members, not far from the total membership of the Independent Labour Party.

What was Unionism?

The issue of Unionism, which had seemed to threaten Liberal unity, also helped pave the way for new ideas. In 1886 Liberal Prime Minister William Gladstone proposed Home Rule for Ireland. What that meant was a form of devolution for Ireland, similar to the powers the Scottish Government has today. However, such a proposal caused some Liberal MPs to resign and move towards the Conservatives. The issue was Unionism. Unionists were people who supported the Union of Scotland, England, Ireland and Wales and were opposed to any attempt to break it up. The immediate effect on the Liberals was damaging. The party split, with many of the older, more traditional Liberals breaking away to form the Liberal Unionists. The Liberal Unionists and Conservatives were formally joined in 1912 to create the Scottish Unionist Party.

Why did the other parties not attract such large support?

The Conservatives were associated with the big landowners and landlords in the towns who in turn were seen to be making huge profits from rents charged for bad-quality housing. The following statement comes from Thomas Johnston who was a Labour supporter, but the tone of its attack on the wealthy struck a cord with many working class Scots. In *Our Scots Noble Families* he declared:

> *Generation after generation, these few families of tax-gatherers, have sucked the lifeblood of our nation. In their prides and lusts they have sent us to war, family against family, clan against clan, race against race. The labouring man has sweated and starved so that they might live in idleness and luxury.*
>
> *Thomas Johnston,* Our Scots Noble Families, *1999 (first published 1909)*

By the end of the nineteenth century the Conservatives (sometimes called Tories) wanted to protect British farming and some industries by putting up tariff barriers against foreign competition. The effect would be to make food from abroad more expensive and might harm British exports abroad. In Scotland, protection was not popular for three reasons. Scottish farmers were not so dependent on wheat prices compared with the south of England, the urban population in Scotland did not want food prices to rise, and Scottish industry was heavily dependant on international trade. The last thing Scottish businesses wanted was anything that would make trade more difficult so Conservative policies were not widely popular in Scotland. In order to win an election before the First World War the Conservatives were dependant on the Liberals losing a significant number of votes to the Labour Party.

What was the Labour Party?

Working-class men in the town and country gained the right to vote in 1884 but there was no working-class party to attract their votes. That started to change in 1888 when the Ayrshire miners' leader James Keir Hardie suggested that he become the Liberal candidate at a by-election in Mid-Lanark. His offer was rejected. Keir Hardie then decided to stand in Mid-Lanark as an independent Labour candidate. Until that point the Liberals had helped to support some working-class MPs who were nicknamed 'LibLabs' but Keir Hardie wanted to be completely independent from the other political parties.

Source 1.9

This cartoon suggests Keir Hardie is mad to cut his Labour Party away from the Liberals. By the end of the war the Labour branch had grown while the Liberal tree had crashed.

NOT A WISE SAW

Mr. Keir Hardie wishes to make Labour representation entirely independent of the Liberal Party.

Although Keir Hardie lost the election, the first steps had been taken in creating a Labour Party in Britain. In the summer of 1888 the Scottish Labour Party was born. It campaigned for better health and safety in the mining industry, the introduction of an eight-hour maximum working day, votes and political rights for women and home rule for Scotland. Keir

Hardie also played a leading role in the formation of the British Independent Labour Party (ILP) in 1893. The following year the Scottish Labour Party merged with the ILP and in 1900 they in turn joined others in the Labour Representation Committee, later to be called the Labour Party.

How important was the Labour Party in Scotland before 1914?

The Labour Party was very new and untested before 1914. The party failed to make any big impression in Scotland before the First World War, with only three Scottish MPs amongst the 42 British MPs in 1910. In fact, by 1914 Labour had only 8 candidates in the national election. Labour had failed to undermine the traditional loyalty of Scottish working-class voters to the Liberals, especially as the Liberals offered policies of wide-ranging social reform. In 1914 it seemed the Labour Party, certainly in Scotland, was almost an irrelevance. The Liberals seemed secure for many years to come and consistently won support from all sections of a society that retained a strong feeling of Scottish identity. Yet within ten years Labour had become, for a short time, the governing party of Britain and the Liberals were in permanent decline. The Great War had a huge effect on the political parties in Britain, as you will find out later in this book.

Scottish identity before the First World War

Source 1.10

Even English biscuits used images of Highlanders when selling their product abroad.

Scotland within Britain

Prior to the First World War, most Scots thought of themselves as British and were happy to be part of Britain and its Empire. Being part of Britain offered Scots many opportunities: Scotland was part of the world's leading industrial and military superpower – Great Britain. Scots shared in the nationalist pride of the British Empire where they saw themselves as equal partners with the English as soldiers, statesmen, engineers and businessmen.

At the same time, throughout the nineteenth century a version of Scottish identity was reinforced by references to Scottish history and brave heroes, nostalgia for the old rural ways, and by a Queen who redefined

'Scottishness' at Balmoral. 'Highlandism' – a tartan and bagpipe image of Scotland – was sold in the pages of Scottish popular magazines such as the *People's Journal* with 250,000 weekly sales. According to Tom Devine:

> 66 *Scots from the Borders, the Lowland cities or the rural counties of the east found that Highland identity was an effective way of confirming their Scottishness… Highlandism had seductive appeal. It allowed for the expression of a truly distinctive Scottish identity that clearly differentiated the nation from England. Highland symbols, customs and beliefs had enormous capacity to project such an image.*
>
> Tom Devine, The Scottish Nation 1700–2007, *2006*

In *Scotland's Empire 1600–1815*, Devine makes the point that 'the kilted battalions, more than any other single factor, popularised Highland dress and made it the national symbol of Scotland' (Devine, *Scotland's Empire 1600–1815*, 2004). The image of Scotland as a loyal and brave part of the United Kingdom was at its most obvious in its army and what became known as Scotland's martial traditions.

Scotland and its martial traditions

Before, during and after the First World War Scottish soldiers were praised for their martial traditions. In simple terms this meant Scottish soldiers were seen as brave, loyal and trustworthy; men who could be relied on to fight to the end for their friends, their regiment and their country.

Why was Scotland thought to have strong martial traditions?

During the war Scottish troops were repeatedly used in the first wave of attack – 'shock troops' to hit the enemy hard, to break through by sheer aggression and to continue the advance by solid determination. Scottish troops were seen to be carrying on the martial tradition of their ancestors.

Until the middle of the eighteenth century Highland Scotland was seen as warlike and a dangerous place, even to lowland Scots. The core of this threat and aggression seemed to lie in the Highland clan system, with male clan members valued for their fighting skills. The Jacobite invasion of England in 1745–46 terrified both lowland Scots and most of England. After the Jacobite defeat at Culloden in 1746 the government wanted to end the concept of clans as fighting units. They took away the power of the clan chiefs and destroyed clan warrior identity by banning the wearing of tartan

and playing of bagpipes. However, the government was keen to recruit Highlanders into the British army and early reports suggested they fought as well for the government as they had for their highland chiefs.

By the middle of the nineteenth century the nightmare of hairy clansmen rampaging into England had been replaced by a new stereotype – the loyal Scottish soldier, a 'kilted hero' of the British Empire. A report from 1773 described the Highland soldier as:

> 66 *Often tried and proved, [they] were always found to be firm and trusty troops. Our commanders [have] the highest confidence in them, and never were they disappointed in them.*

Between 1777 and 1800 the Highlands produced more than 20 regiments for the British army. Highland soldiers were given new chiefs within the army, they wore the kilt officially adopted as part of their uniform and marched to the sound of bagpipes wherever they were sent to expand the British Empire. The UK government had turned the features that made the Scottish clansmen such fierce enemies into British military traditions. In Britain, paintings, plays, official biographies, regimental histories and even, eventually, children's comics all created an image of the brave Scottish soldier defending the Empire against any threat. As the Empire grew so did the need for soldiers and Highland landowners were only too happy to take advantage of government incentives to recruit men from their estates.

Martial race ideology

When Charles Darwin wrote his *Origin of Species* he argued that the 'survival of the fittest' was a central point in understanding why some species survived and others did not. Very quickly new racial theories grew up along similar lines. These racial theories argued that some races were more intelligent, more aggressive or more hardworking than others. Nowadays such racist ideas have been discredited but in the middle of the nineteenth century military leaders firmly believed in the martial race theory.

They believed that certain races or groups of people were naturally more warlike and aggressive in battle, and that they possessed qualities such as courage, loyalty, strength and a willingness to work hard. The UK government believed that the Scottish Highland warriors were exactly what it needed! Tom Devine explains:

> *Before, the Gael [Highlander] was alien and racially inferior; now, the exploits of the Highland soldier made him a standard bearer for long held beliefs about the martial virtues of the Scottish nation.*

Tom Devine, *The Scottish Nation 1700–2007, 2006, page 240*

Source 1.11

Highlanders defending the British Empire – 'The Thin Red Line' was an iconic image from the Crimean War.

The power of the tartan

In the nineteenth century the publication of supposedly ancient poems by Ossian gloried in the bravery and virtues of long-ago Highland warriors. The stories of Sir Walter Scott added to the romantic image of the Highland warrior. Finally, Queen Victoria's royal approval and patronage of the Highlands generally and the Highland regiments put the kilted Scottish soldier at the very peak of tartan 'Highlandism' in the later-nineteenth century. The whole of Scotland seemed to be condensed into the public image of the Highlands while Highland societies, both in Britain and abroad, celebrated past glories and revived 'historic' traditions. The power of the tartan-clad soldier was such that in 1881 the War Office ordered even lowland regiments to wear tartan trews (trousers).

Tradition, recruitment and casualties

When war broke out in 1914 recruitment often focused on the heroism and past deeds of the Highland men, and, of course, the pressure on them not to let down their ancestors and family traditions. Even the supposed unbroken link between clan warriors and clan chief was reborn in the appeals for men to join the army in 1914. The link between Highlandism, militarism and the Scottish military tradition was stretched even further by references to past victories won by Highland troops. On 12 March 1915, in an article entitled 'What the Hebrides has done', the *Inverness Courier* wrote:

> *The virtue of patriotism in them is not a growth of yesterday. It is a noble heritage from a race of ancestors whose deeds of valour [bravery] on continental fields find a prominent place in the pages of history.*

Inverness Courier, *1915*

The powerful image of the Highland warrior lived on into the trenches of the Great War. In 1916 an English soldier, Ernest Parker, wrote:

> *One thing I shall never forget is the sight of thousands of rhythmically swinging kilts as a Highland Division swept towards us. Skirling at the head of the column strode the pipers, filing the air with their wild martial music. Behind glinted a forest of rifle barrels. These men seemed a crack military unit ready to carry out its mission.*

Quoted in Trevor Royle, The Flowers of the Forest: Scotland and the Great War, *2006, page 51*

By the end of the war, over a quarter of the 557,000 Scottish men who had joined up had been killed or injured. In the rest of the British army the death rate had been 11 per cent. The Scottish casualty rate of 26 per cent put Scotland into the top three countries who had suffered most in the conflict. Only Serbia and Turkey suffered more but their casualties had been made much worse by disease – Scottish casualties were solely the result of fighting. Perhaps the belief in the Scots' military traditions of bravery and determination and ties of loyalty to family and clan was indeed an important factor leading to the horrendous 'butcher's bill' of the Great War paid by Scotland.

Source 1.12

The 51st Highland Division war memorial at Bruar, in Perthshire.

Activities

Scotland in 1914

Your challenge is to produce a display or presentation showing the main features of Scotland in 1914 as they apply to your course of study.

Your display or presentation must make people want to stop and look at your views of Scotland in 1914.

Work in a group of no more than four. Your teacher will give you an appropriate time scale for the task.

Special Note: Store your display in a safe place. You will do a similar exercise at the end of this course and you will be asked to compare the two displays and reach conclusions about the impact of the Great War on Scotland.

Your display or presentation should deal with the following topics:

- Scottish identity
- Scots abroad
- Scottish industry
- Scottish politics
- Scottish lowland life
- Scottish highland life
- Scottish military traditions.

continued

Success criteria

Somewhere in your display or presentation each topic should have:

- a four sentence text box explaining your ideas
- one illustration – or two if you want to show differing points of view
- a smart slogan summarising the core issue associated with the topic.

Your display must be visible across a classroom. It must use at least three colours and must use at least two different sizes of text. Think creatively – who said it has to be paper based?

Scotland and the Impact of the Great War 1914–1928

2 Scots on the Western Front

On 4 August 1914 Britain joined the Great War. Not until later was it necessary to identify world wars by numbers and call it the First World War.

Tension in Europe

Source 2.1

How does this pre-war cartoon illustrate the tensions and aggressions in Europe before 1914?

Tension had been building in Europe for some time. The arrival of Kaiser Wilhelm II on the German throne in 1888 began a period of instability in Europe and by 1914 European powers were divided into competing alliances, often described as two armed camps. On one side the Triple Alliance of Germany, Austria–Hungary and Italy faced the Triple Entente of France, Russia and Great Britain.

Plans and alliances

Suspicion and jealousy fuelled international tension before 1914, so much so that secret war plans were made by each of the major powers, each one hoping to launch a successful 'first strike' on their enemies. Germany,

trapped between France and Russia, created the Schlieffen Plan. The Schlieffen Plan aimed to launch a massive attack through neutral Belgium, catch France unprepared, capture Paris and then accept France's surrender – all within six weeks. The Germans anticipated that Russia would take about six weeks to launch its own attacks and they planned to attack Russia before it was ready to respond.

Meanwhile Britain had no recent alliances. It did have friendly agreements with France and Russia but that was all. Some military planning had taken place between Britain and France but Britain clung to the belief that it was safe as an island protected by its huge Dreadnought battleships.

The Balkan spark

The spark that ignited the Great War was struck in the Balkans, an area of tension in south-eastern Europe. Both Russia and Austria–Hungary wanted to control the Balkans. The largest Balkan country, Serbia, wanted to increase its power and also protect its independence. Serbia believed Russia would help it and also believed Austria–Hungary was its enemy.

Source 2.2

The Great Powers crowd together on top of the boiling pot of the Balkans. How does this cartoon illustrate the growing concern over Balkan issues before 1914?

BALKAN TROUBLES

THE BOILING POINT.

When Arch Duke Franz Ferdinand, heir to the Austro–Hungarian throne, was assassinated on 28 June 1914, a spark was lit that would explode over Europe. Austria–Hungary blamed Serbia for helping the assassins. In reality, Austria–Hungary was looking for an excuse to weaken Serbia, possibly by war. To protect itself Serbia called in favours from Russia. At the same time Austria–Hungary made sure it had backing from its ally Germany. By the end of July 1914 the two armed camps were ready to march into war. Once Germany declared its support for Austria–Hungary, France declared its support for Russia. Germany, faced with the prospect of fighting a war on two fronts, launched its Schlieffen Plan and German troops advanced into Belgium.

Britain, Belgium and the scrap of paper

In 1839 Britain, along with other European powers, had signed the Treaty of London. It guaranteed that no country would attack or move any troops into Belgium without its permission. When Germany invaded Belgium in 1914, 75 years after the Treaty of London was signed, the Kaiser did not believe any country would bother about the Treaty of London and called it a 'scrap of paper'. However, Britain did decide to support Belgium. Later historians argue that the treaty was a convenient excuse for Britain to enter into war with its major European competitor and that Britain had wanted war for some time. Either way, on 4 August 1914, Britain declared war on Germany. On that same day the leading article in *The Scotsman* newspaper stated:

> *Belgium has resolved to stand by her liberties at all risks knowing that she has Britain behind her. If we allow Belgian rights to be forcibly overridden at this time, it would be our turn to fall victims to the greed and ambition of Germany.*
>
> *Quoted in Trevor Royle,* The Flowers of the Forest: Scotland and the Great War, 2006, *pages 23–24*

The problem was that Britain did not have an army capable of fighting a long war!

The British Army in 1914

In 1914 the British army was entirely voluntary. The soldiers were called regulars – volunteers who had joined the army and agreed to serve for a number of years. Regulars were professional soldiers who were mostly working-class men, led by more wealthy and better-educated middle-class or upper-class officers. Volunteers joined regiments they were familiar with and that often meant the regiment that was identified with the local area. For example, the Royal Scots tended to attract volunteers from Edinburgh while Borders men joined the King's Own Scottish Borderers (KOSB) and men from Aberdeenshire joined the Gordon Highlanders. However, it was also quite normal for men to travel across the country to join regiments of their choice.

Soldiers identified strongly with their regiment. John Baynes of the 2nd Scottish Rifles wrote:

> " *By the time the men had lived for two or three years in the Regimental tradition, they had made the strongest friendships of their lives and the Regiment could claim them as its own.*
>
> *Quoted in Royle,* The Flowers of the Forest: Scotland and the Great War, *2006, page 50*

The British Expeditionary Force

The British Expeditionary Force (BEF) was the title given to the forces of the British Army sent from Great Britain to fight in France and Belgium in the opening months of the First World War. The BEF was described by the army's official historian, James Edmonds, as 'the best trained, best organised, and best equipped British Army which ever went to war'. (Quoted in Royle, *The Fowers of the Forest: Scotland and the Great War*, 2006). The BEF faced the first impact of the war and had 90,000 casualties by the end of 1914.

The BEF was very small in comparison to the armies of its French allies and its German enemies but the rifle-firing skill of its soldiers allowed it 'to punch above its weight' in the early battles of 1914. Within a week of the war starting the German army had **four million** soldiers and on 19 August Kaiser Wilhelm II allegedly ordered his troops to 'walk over Britain's contemptible little army'. Ever since then the BEF has been nicknamed the 'Old Contemptibles'.

Source 2.3

Can you explain the connection between the illustration and the purpose of this poster?

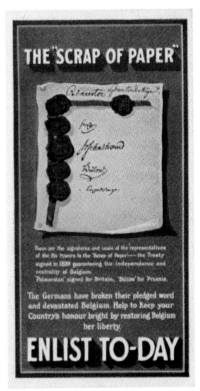

By late 1914 and early 1915 the BEF had suffered so many casualties that there was a danger that Britain would be unable to keep fighting. Kitchener's New Army of volunteers (see page 27, 'Creating an army') was not yet ready to fight so it was the Territorials who kept Britain in the war by 'plugging the gap'.

The Territorial Army

The Territorial Army was started in 1908. These 'part-time' soldiers signed up for four years. The men joining the Territorials could identify with units linked to their workplace or where they lived. Volunteers attended locally-based evening drills and an annual summer camp where they received basic military training.

The Territorial Army had evolved from volunteer rifle regiments formed in the nineteenth century. Volunteer regiments had been very popular in Scotland. They allowed local men to wear uniforms, do military training and feel they were helping protect their country while at the same time avoiding regular army life. By 1913 over 245,000 men were in the Territorial Army but they did not have to serve oversees unless they had agreed to it when they signed up. Just over 20,000 men had done so but when war broke out almost all the Territorials agreed to serve wherever they were needed.

The Territorials were to play a vital part in the war but when Kitchener became Secretary of State for War he did not trust Territorial discipline or combat readiness. He felt that too many of the Territorials, especially the officers, had joined only for the social life.

In contrast to Kitchener's views on the Territorials, the author John Buchan described the Territorials in his book *Mr Standfast*, written in 1919, as:

 Scottish Territorials. Mostly clerks and shop men and engineers and farmer's sons. They are super-excellent and consequently so are the officers. They get top marks in the Boche (German) calendar for sheer fighting devilment.

John Buchan, Mr. Standfast, 2008 (first published 1919)

Buchan was correct. When war broke out almost as many men joined the Territorial Army as Kitchener's New Army and Territorial units fought bravely, filling the gap in the high casualty lists of the BEF until Kitchener's New Army of volunteers could be used in France.

The BEF goes to war

The BEF began moving across to France on Monday 10 August 1914. George Ramage of the Gordon Highlanders wrote in his diary:

> 66 *After crossing the English Channel to France, our ship dropped anchor about 5a.m. at the mouth of the river Seine. On the left side of the shore on huge signs were the words "God bless you all" in big letters. French obviously grateful and in need of British help. Saw first French soldier in blue coat and baggy red trousers – he waved a salute from the shore. People on shore waved hands and cheered – men on boats and shouted "Hooray" and their boats hooted a welcome. Flags on nearly all the buildings – many Union Jacks. "Heep, heep, Hooray" they shout and "Welcome to France."*

From the diary of George Ramage

Source 2.4

Members of a battalion of the London Scottish regiment on parade, taken in 1915.

Source 2.5

Douglas Hepburn of the London Scottish, aged 18 in 1915.

Once they arrived in France the troops were given rifle practice and daily route marches with full packs to bring them up to fighting fitness. Private Douglas Hepburn of the London Scottish wrote in a letter home:

 My Dear Ma,

Arrived at our base all right after having a merciless ride of 18 hours in a "French Train". Well, we got to our destination at 2a.m., had something to eat and then at 5a.m. had some tea. We have not been slacking during our time at Rouen. Every morning bayonet and squad drill, practising and charging at dummies, shooting as well with live bullets.

From the author's private collection

Soon afterwards Hepburn and the others in the BEF marched on to face the enemy.

Creating an army

The British government had not expected to fight a land-based European war. Instead, it had expected the land war to be fought by French and Russian armies while Britain defeated Germany at sea. The government also expected a short war, hopefully 'over by Christmas'. Members of the government were therefore shocked when the new Secretary of State for War, Field-Marshal Lord Kitchener, stated that Britain would need a million men to defeat Germany and it would take at least three years to do it.

Kitchener immediately began a recruiting campaign by calling for men aged between 19 and 30 to join the British Army. Three weeks later he raised the recruiting age to 35.

The recruitment poster in Source 2.6 shows Kitchener declaring 'Your Country needs you' and has become an international icon. As Margot Asquith, wife of Prime Minister Herbert Asquith, said at the time, 'He may not be a great man, but he makes a great poster'.

In Scotland, thousands of young and not-so-young men volunteered to fight for their country as soon as war was declared. There were more Scots volunteers in proportion to the size of the population than any other area of UK. Kitchener stated:

 I feel certain that Scotsmen have only to know that their country urgently needs their service for them to offer with the same splendid patriotism as they have always shown in the past... Their services were never more needed than they are today and that I rely confidently on a splendid response to the national appeal.

Quoted in Trevor Royle, The Flowers of the Forest: *Scotland and the Great War, 2006, page 31*

Scots on the Western Front

Source 2.6

Possibly the most famous poster of all time – the first to use the optical illusion of the finger pointing at YOU. Try moving the book so it does NOT point at you!

Kitchener was not disappointed. He asked for 100,000 volunteers, hoping to train a new army of over a million men by 1917. The *Daily Record* newspaper reported that within 'two days of war starting and over the first weekend of war, 6000 men from all classes enlisted in Glasgow' (Quoted in Macdonald and McFarland, *Scotland and the Great War*, 1998, page 61). By the end of August 20,000 men had signed up at the Gallowgate in Glasgow. In Alloa 750 men joined and at Dumbarton just under 1000 men joined the army. By September 1914 Kitchener had his 100,000 men but more kept volunteering. On one day in October 1914 over 35,000 men from across the UK enlisted in the army for the duration of the war and by the middle of September over 500,000 men had volunteered their services. It was reported that men determined to join up were ready to say anything and sign anything and that they gave false names, false addresses and false ages in order to do so.

Kitchener's campaign was a huge success. By the end of 1914 almost 24 per cent of the entire male labour force in western Scotland had joined up and the *Dundee Advertiser* had declared 'all honour to the lads who have put Scotland in the front this time. We must not let the sons of the Rose or the Leek or the Shamrock get in front of the proud Thistle.' (Quoted in Macdonald and McFarland, *Scotland and the Great War*, 1998, page 61)

Why did so many young men rush to join the army?

Why was voluntary recruitment so high? Was it a wave of mass hysteria that made young Scots rush to join the army? Recent research has shown there were many reasons to join up, including a desire to quit a boring or difficult job, take a chance of seeing another country or to escape family troubles.

At first the outbreak of war was exciting. The opportunity to go on an adventure with your pals in a kilties uniform was too good to miss. As grocery shop assistant Robert Irvine said, 'I was only a shop assistant at the time. I wanted to escape from the humdrum life behind [the] grocery counter and see a bit of the country.' (Quoted in Young, *Scottish Voices from the Great War*, 2005, page 24)

The war was not expected to last long and there was a chance that if you did not join up then you might miss the fun. The possibility of facing death or serious injury was put aside. One soldier said, looking back on the foolish innocence of 1914, 'the folk at hame never said a word to disuade me. We all had a pathetic faith that we should come through somehow'.

Source 2.7

Posters used all sorts of emotional pressures to get men to join up. How does this poster work?

War hysteria also played a part in recruitment. Even fairly sensible writers were affected by stories of spies and German wickedness. Neil Munro wrote, 'There were already guards on reservoirs and railway bridges. Their [the German's] readiness to poison us at our kitchen taps was taken for

granted.' (Quoted in Royle, *The Flowers of the Forest: Scotland and the Great War*, 2006, page 25)

During the first few months of the war the War Propaganda Bureau published pamphlets such as the 'Report on Alleged German Outrages' that seemed to give official proof that the German Army had systematically tortured Belgian civilians. Stories of babies being bayoneted, their heads used as footballs, and nurses and nuns being raped were often told as truth.

Sunset Song, by Lewis Grassic Gibbon, is a novel set in the north-east of Scotland in the early twentieth century which reflects the spirit of rural Scotland at the time. It describes the moment when news of the outbreak of war reached the village of Kinraddie and sums up how many people felt when they heard of the 'Belgian Atrocities'.

> *One night in the mid days of August as they sat at meat, the door burst open and in strode Chae Strachan, a paper in his hand and was fell excited. Chris listened. A war was on and Britain was at war with Germany... Chae told them every man might yet have to fight for bairn and wife ere this war was over; and he said that the Germans had broken loose and were raping women and braining bairns all over Belgium.*

> *Lewis Grassic Gibbon,* Sunset Song, *1996 (first published 1932)*

Most Scots believed the stories of atrocities and joined up to save civilisation or just to punish the Germans. Very few Scots took the view of Charles Hamilton Sorley who had spent some time studying in Germany. He wrote, 'I wish the silly papers would realise they [the Germans] are fighting for a principle just as much as we are.' (Quoted in Royle, *The Flowers of the Forest: Scotland and the Great War*, 2006, page 27).

Peer pressure, cranked up by newspapers, also played a part in recruitment. One soldier wrote, 'my parents would have been ashamed of me had I not done so'. Tramcars were used as recruiting stations and toured the suburbs of cities. In the Highlands, old clan loyalties and the fighting traditions of the Highland soldier were used as recruiting levers. The *Inverness Courier* wrote:

> *The country still appeals for men. The call has gone forth to those straths and glens from where were drawn the warriors who fought under Wellington in the Peninsula [against Napoleon in Spain from 1808–1812] and took a notable part in upholding their country's honour in Belgium [Battle of Waterloo, 1815] a few years later.*

> *Quoted in Catriona Macdonald and Elaine McFarland,* Scotland and the Great War, *1998, page 86*

In the lowlands, football loyalties became a target for recruitment, especially in the first few months of the war when thousands of young men who had not joined up were seen crowding into matches. Newspaper articles at the time suggested that football clubs should forget about their profits and instead encourage their players and supporters to join up.

One team in particular, Heart of Midlothian, has long been associated with its support for the war effort. By late 1914 Hearts had suffered only one defeat in sixteen League games. Three players were in the forces, but general recruitment was slowing and public opinion was moving firmly against the playing of football while men suffered on the battlefields. Sir George McCrae, a volunteer soldier, obtained permission to raise and command a new battalion in Edinburgh – the 16th Royal Scots. His recruitment drive was given a huge boost when thirteen Hearts players signed up. In six days, 600 Hearts supporters helped to form 'McCrae's Battalion' of 1350 officers and men. At the Christmas pantomime at the Kings Theatre, Edinburgh, in 1914, a verse was read out:

> *Do not ask where Hearts are playing and then look at me askance,*
> *If it's football that you're wanting you must come with us to France*

Quoted in Trevor Royle, The Flowers of the Forest: Scotland and the Great War, *2006, page 34*

Source 2.8

By 1916 these members of Hearts football team were hardened veterans of the war.

TEAM 1914–15

For some recruits, joining the army might not have been entirely voluntary. Some historians argue, perhaps rather cynically, that fear of unemployment was probably as great a reason for joining up as patriotic enthusiasm and solidarity with brave little Belgium. Research into employment figures shows that army recruitment among coal miners in the East Lothian coalfields, hit by a collapse of trade, was as high as 36 per cent, while at the same time only 20 per cent joined from the still-prosperous Ayrshire coal fields. More research into the sentencing of guilty criminals at Scottish city courts found that prison sentences fell hugely in 1914 compared with 1913 because the guilty were often 'persuaded' to volunteer to enlist.

At the beginning of the war the army had strict specifications about who could become a soldier. Men joining the army had to be at least 5 feet 6 inches tall and have a chest measurement of 35 inches. Some historians have argued that as the recruiting sergeant and the medical examining doctor were each paid a reward for every recruit they signed up, there was a huge incentive to turn a blind eye to volunteers who might not quite meet the correct height, weight or age requirements.

The Earl of Wemyss had a more direct way of enforcing recruitment. He declared that:

 Every able bodied man [aged] 18–30 at present working on my estates will be put on half pay for the duration of the war and their jobs kept open on condition that they join up. If they do not enlist they will be compelled to leave my employment.

The Earl of Wemyss

In conclusion, there are many and varied reasons for Scottish voluntary recruitment in 1914–1915. Certainly the virtues of heroism, self sacrifice, honour and patriotism played a big part. Young men who thought they would look good in a kilt and Glengarry also wanted to escape the boredom and drudgery of their work and their lives. The attraction of adventure and excitement was strong. There was a tradition of respect for the military in Scotland and, to those who had been unemployed or were unskilled, the army offered a steady wage. Even after the casualty lists lengthened in 1915, recruitment in Scotland remained higher than many other parts of Britain.

The Scottish 'Pals'

The 'Pals battalions' were units of the British Army that consisted of men who had volunteered together on the promise that they would be able to serve alongside their mates rather than being scattered in different units of the army. Although the name 'Pals battalion' was not officially recognised in

Scotland, the idea that volunteers who joined together would stay together was evident in Glasgow, where four battalions were raised, and in Edinburgh, where three were raised. There were also four Tyneside Scottish 'Pals'.

By the summer of 1916 there were 215 locally-raised battalions across the UK. The idea of the 'Pals battalions' was an attempt to help Kitchener get all the volunteers he needed. Sir Henry Rawlinson suggested that men would be more inclined to enlist in the army if they knew that they were going to serve alongside their friends and workmates. This was not a new idea. The Territorial Army was based on exactly the same appeal of fighting alongside friends, neighbours and workmates.

In Glasgow the 15th (City of Glasgow) Battalion of the Highland Light Infantry was known as the Tramway Battalion because most of the original members belonged to the city's transport department. At first the men of the Tramway Battalion had no uniform to wear so they paraded through Glasgow in their green transport department uniforms following a pipe band.

Likewise, the 16th Battalion was known as the Boys Brigade, made up of members of that organisation, while the 17th Battalion was created from members of Glasgow's Chamber of Commerce. Glasgow's final 'Pals battalion' was a bantam battalion raised in 1915. These were men who had initially been rejected for the army because they were less than 5 feet 6 inches tall.

Edinburgh could not sit back and let Glasgow seize the glory of raising its own battalions so Cranston's Battalion and McCrae's Battalions were raised from local men and became part of the Royal Scots. Later, Edinburgh also raised a bantam battalion. The most famous of the locally-raised battalions was the 16th (2nd Edinburgh) Battalion, raised by McCrae, because of its connection with Hearts Football Club. The entire first and reserve teams, several boardroom and staff members and many of the club's supporters all joined McRae's Battalion.

The idea of friends going to war together had many attractions but it was also a recipe for disaster. Nobody seems to have thought what would happen if a Pals battalion went into action and suffered heavy casualties. The effect on the area the Pals came from would be devastating. That was what happened at the Battle of the Somme when the Glasgow Boys Brigade Battalion went into battle. More than 500 young men, all of who were connected to the Boys Brigade and came from the same network of Glasgow streets, were killed. The monument to their regiment – the 51st Highland Light Infantry – at Beaumont Hammel on the Somme battlefield reads, 'Friends are good on the day of battle'. It was friendship that led them to join together – and die together. After the losses at the Somme, and particularly after conscription was introduced, all thought of keeping pals together was abandoned.

Activities

The date is October 1914. You volunteered for the army in August 1914.

The army needs more volunteers and you have been asked to return to your home town to make a speech to encourage other young men to join up. You are asked to inspire and enthuse the men listening to you. How will you achieve your target in a speech lasting no less than two minutes?

Or

The date is October 1914. You volunteered for the army in August 1914.

The army needs more volunteers and you have been asked to write an article for your local newspaper. You are asked to inspire and enthuse the men who read your article. How will you achieve your target in an article of no more than 250 words?

Or

Prepare and deliver a presentation to your class explaining why so many young Scottish men joined the armed forces in the autumn of 1914. Your presentation should provide context background, factual detail and a clear list of the various reasons. Your presentation must last between four and five minutes.

The Western Front – over by Christmas?

When war broke out most military planners expected troops to move quite quickly, big battles to be fought and the war to be over around Christmas time. When German troops swept into Belgium as part of the Schlieffen Plan it appeared that the expectations of a swift, short war of movement would be met. Almost nobody planned for the stalemate of the Western Front. Only General Kitchener, who was made Secretary of War in the British Government, thought differently. He told the Prime Minister that it would take at least three years to defeat Germany, at the cost of millions of casualties.

When the BEF arrived in France they advanced towards the German forces. They slowed the German advance at Mons but still had to retreat. The Germans pushed on but soon the Schlieffen Plan began to unravel. Belgian resistance and the actions of the BEF caused the German advance to become ragged and it was stopped at the river Marne. French and British troops forced the Germans to retreat – the Schlieffen Plan had failed.

Source 2.9

The Western Front

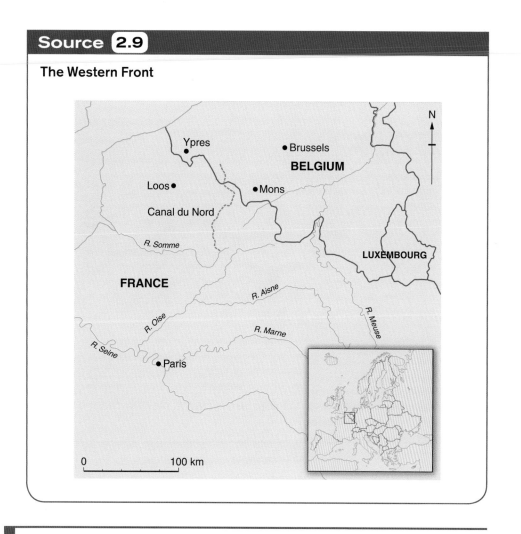

The start of trench warfare

The Germans only retreated until they found good positions where they could 'dig in' and build defensive trenches. Trenches were not new; they had been used extensively in the American Civil War and in the Crimean War earlier in the mid-nineteenth century. A basic trench was simply a deep ditch dug by soldiers to protect themselves and make it easier to defend their position.

Naturally when British and French forces met the German defences they also dug trenches to protect themselves. Each side tried to break through and outflank their enemy but all that happened was that each side dug more trenches to widen their defensive front.

Eventually both sides had dug defensive lines stretching 400 miles from the English Channel to the Swiss border. The Western Front had become deadlocked into trench warfare.

Source 2.10

How many reasons can you se in this drawing to explain why the trench systems would not be broken by attack easily?

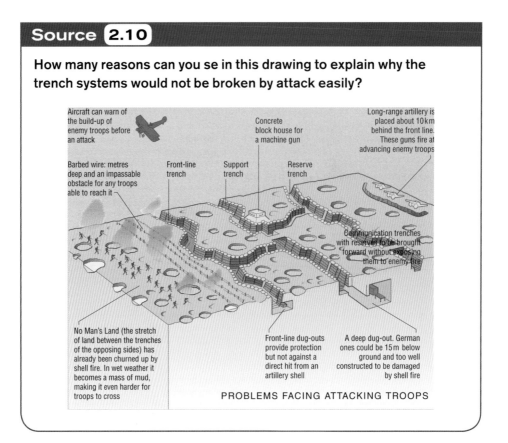

Aircraft can warn of the build-up of enemy troops before an attack

Concrete block house for a machine gun

Long-range artillery is placed about 10 km behind the front line. These guns fire at advancing enemy troops

Barbed wire: metres deep and an impassable obstacle for any troops able to reach it

Front-line trench

Support trench

Reserve trench

Communication trenches with reserves to be brought forward without exposing them to enemy fire

No Man's Land (the stretch of land between the trenches of the opposing sides) has already been churned up by shell fire. In wet weather it becomes a mass of mud, making it even harder for troops to cross

Front-line dug-outs provide protection but not against a direct hit from an artillery shell

A deep dug-out. German ones could be 15 m below ground and too well constructed to be damaged by shell fire

PROBLEMS FACING ATTACKING TROOPS

For most of the next four years neither side managed to gain a decisive breakthrough. For the British soldiers the real problem with the trench system was that their trenches were almost always in a weaker position than those of the enemy. Douglas Hepburn was an ordinary soldier in the London Scottish. He wrote home in December 1914:

> *Their front line trench was on the edge of a crest – they were able to see for miles around while our front line was in a dip, we being able to see very little.*
>
> *The author's private collection*

A few weeks later he described what they found when a British attack forced a German unit to retreat:

> *We had our signal station in the cellar of a big house where the Germans had been before. By gum! They knew how to make themselves comfortable. There were beds down there, a mirror at the side, chairs and a table, curtains hung over the bed and a lot of empty bottles piled in a corner.*
>
> *The author's private collection*

Deadlock

Fairly soon both sides had created networks of well-defended deep trenches. Barbed wire and machine-gun fire made defence relatively easy but made attack so much more difficult. As each side pounded the other with artillery it made the landscape so much more difficult to attack over. In the low-lying area of Flanders artillery barrages destroyed the natural drainage and with heavy rain the whole area became a huge bog. On 28 December 1915 Douglas Hepburn described not only the mud and wet but also how close the German front line was:

There is hardly any news to relate from the trenches, nothing special happened on Christmas Day, only that all of us "got the wind up" about what the Germans were up to. I never spent a more rotten three days in the front line. The barbed wire is not more than thirty yards apart where we were. Last night while I was on guard I heard the Germans whistling and shouting to each other between the hours of twelve and one. They sounded in very high spirits. Last Sunday I was in L......... In parts the roads were absolutely under water and everything is covered in slosh or seems to be.

The author's private collection

It is a cliché to think that soldiers arrived at the trenches and lived in these holes in the ground for four years. Boredom, disease, lice and rats were problems but less so than stories have suggested. The overall impression that soldiers suffered an unending nightmare in the trenches is false. In January 1915 the longest continuous time a Black Watch soldier spent in the front-line trenches was four days. No matter how bad conditions were in front-line trenches on a Monday, a soldier knew that, usually, by Friday he would be behind his lines; warm, fed and safe. Only by this system of organised rotation of troops was morale kept up. Troops were rotated between front-line positions and billets in the rear. There simply was not room in the trench for a whole division!

Dead bodies did not lie unburied near the trenches. The Army command was worried about disease so burial units were always at work. Food scraps were also discouraged and rats were seldom a major problem. However, lice were a problem, as Private Hepburn explained:

August 9, 1915
I have started with the powder you sent. The itching I have experienced during the past two or three days has been absolutely terrible. It makes me go nearly mad.

The author's private collection

Scots on the Western Front

When troops were moved back from the front line uniforms were debugged, washed, ironed and exchanged if too badly infested. However, the fact remains that thousands of soldiers were eating, sleeping, fighting and dying in holes in the ground. Many soldiers did become disillusioned as the war dragged on and casualties mounted.

Trench warfare was very different from trench life. Although the defenders always had the advantage, nothing would break the stalemate on the Western Front unless change was made to happen. That would only happen if one side attacked the other and tried to break through their lines.

Private Hepburn described such an attack in October 1915:

 The Germans at the point where we attacked were ready and too strong for us. It was on a road we made the attack, the Germans on one side and as we rushed up the other side to the edge the machine gun was turned on us and therefore the casualties. In the morning we came back and the sight of the field was rotten. It was a typical battlefield – see all the dead bodies lying about in different positions, all our own men of course, especially just in front of the German's barbed wire. To see thousands of our troops, stretching right across the plain to the horizon, and stretcher bearers going here and there, doing their work and the wounded absolutely crying for the bearers. It was a sight that could not easily be forgotten on that grey, misty and damp morning.

The author's private collection

Letters from soldiers can be useful sources about trench warfare because of their honesty, as in the example from Private Hepburn. George Ramage was another soldier who wrote honestly and directly about the reality of the war. His diary shows some of the disillusionment and cynicism felt by many soldiers as the war dragged on:

 Charges at one spot or over the whole line are no damned use. Too many lives are lost. As we advance from trench to trench our bombs and ammunition fail [run out] while the enemy is getting closer to his supply. Hence he is sure to recapture some of the trenches we take from him. Perhaps one brilliant piece of generalship will crumple up the line of the Germans. But have we seen any brilliant allied strategy during this war? Perhaps the Germans have trenches all the way back to their own land – they are so methodical. If they have, we may drive them back in a million years.

From the diary of George Ramage

Most letters home were censored and when they were in battle zones soldiers could only send the briefest of pre-printed postcards but clearly some uncensored mail got through! Both Ramage and Hepburn comment on censorship and both got into trouble for not obeying the rules. As Ramage suggests, letters home were used sometimes to mislead the public's view of what was happening by including some less-than-subtle propaganda:

 May 6, 1915

A letter I wrote failed to pass the censor, Lieutenant Thom, because I wrote of lice, wire entanglements and expressed the opinion that Germany had won the war to date and that we were acting wholly defensively on our part of the line. The lieutenant said my letter might alarm some of the people at home. They're not worth fighting for if they are so easily alarmed.

[My officer] suggested I might in my letters put in a story about a wounded German begging water off a British soldier – he wanted me to suggest that the Germans were a cringing lot. He said officers had orders to suppress any details that might discourage recruiting.

From the diary of George Ramage

Private Hepburn knew of the restrictions but still he managed to get into trouble, perhaps not surprising given the detail he put into his letters. Hepburn tried to explain to his parents:

 By the way, please don't publish any more letters of mine as our sergeant has warned me and also says that they should never have been passed by the censor – names of places and regiments – well, enough said there.

The author's private collection

But Hepburn kept sending news! On 17 September 1915 he wrote:

 The battalion is in action again. Came in last night through mud and slosh. Heavy shell and shrapnel are bursting all around us. We will be leaving here soon and going into action again for they are making all sorts of preparations for a "big move". Well, you just keep an eye on the papers for the next three weeks or so and see if there will be any good news from round about the place I have been sending photos of. There is one coming by this post too! (Enough said).

The author's private collection

The battle Hepburn was referring to become known to the world as the Battle of Loos.

The Battle of Loos

To Scottish families then and even now, Loos was a Scottish battlefield. 35,000 Scots took part in the attack and half of the 72 infantry battalions involved had Scottish names. Out of **21,000** dead, one-third was from Scottish regiments. Almost every town and village in Scotland was affected by the losses at Loos. The failure of the attack became a symbol of the shattered Allied hopes of 1915. When referring to the casualty figures after the battle it was said that England's loss was national while Scotland's was personal.

The Battle of Loos has been described as an unnecessary and unwanted battle. The French wanted the British to attack at Loos to divert German forces away from the French who were planning their own attack. British commanders did not agree. They knew Kitchener's new armies were not yet fully trained and wanted to wait until 1916 before launching these new armies into attacks. General Haig, who was to be in charge of the battle, had serious worries about the area of attack. His armies would have to advance over land that he described as flat and almost completely devoid of any cover. The attacking British forces would be in full view of German machine gunners. Despite this, the French still wanted the British attack to go ahead and appealed directly to Kitchener, who was himself under pressure to do all he could to encourage British and French co-operation. He agreed the attack should go ahead.

The Battle of Loos in September 1915 is famous for being the first time the British Army used poison gas as a weapon. When German troops had used gas one year earlier the Allies condemned such wickedness. Now that Britain had the technology to use gas themselves, Haig planned to release chlorine from canisters but the plan was dependent on a steady wind blowing towards the Germans!

Source 2.11

British infantry advancing through gas at the Battle of Loos in 1915.

Haig planned to attack with six divisions. Three were from the regular army, mostly made up from Scottish battalions, including the Black Watch, the Cameron Highlanders, the Highland Light Infantry, the Cameronians, the Argyll and Sutherland Highlanders, Scots Fusiliers and Gordon Highlanders. Another was a Territorial Army division and the other two were made up entirely of volunteers – the 9th and 15th Scottish.

Loos was the first time Kitchener's armies of volunteers had been used in a major attack. On the night before the attack Ted Jackson of the Cameron Highlanders remembered:

 Instead of going to rest for a few hours we gathered in groups talking over our chances in the morning. We commenced singing. All the old favourites were sung one by one, bringing back memories of training days, and old scenes of sunny, southern England. Then friends wished each other "good luck", friends who knew that the next day would find many of them in the casualty list.

Quoted in Trevor Royle, The Flowers of the Forest: Scotland and the Great War, *2006, page 86*

The battle began on 25 September 1915, after a four-day artillery bombardment. A report from the time described how:

> The British started bombarding on the Wednesday and continued till Saturday morning about 5.30. The bombardment was terrific, night and day. Hundreds of guns poured shells on to the enemy lines, the first line of trenches was completely obliterated, and the second and third suffered badly. About 5.30 a.m. on the 25th we sent over our gas, but our boys seemed to be too anxious as they did not give the gas time to travel far enough, and consequently they made up on it before it reached the enemies lines, and a good number went down with it.

There is some confusion about the effectiveness of the gas attack. Some reports suggest the force of the artillery bombardment stopped the gas crossing to the German positions, others suggest the wind changed and blew back in the faces of the attacking Scots. The 10th Highland Light Infantry were gassed as they waited to go 'ower the bags', a phrase used by Scots meaning to attack or go over the top. Further along the front line the King's Own Scottish Borderers prepared to advance but were held up by the gas and shellfire. It looked like the attack might fail until Piper Daniel Laidlaw climbed onto the parapet.

Laidlaw later described what happened:

> At 6.30 the bugles sounded the advance and I got over the parapet with Lieutenant Young. I at once got the pipes going and the laddies gave a cheer as they started off for the enemy's lines. As soon as they showed themselves over the trench top they began to fall fast, but they never wavered, but dashed straight on as I played the old tune they all knew 'Blue Bonnets over the Border'. I ran forward with them piping for all I knew, and just as we were getting near the German lines I was wounded by shrapnel in the left ankle and leg. I was too excited to feel the pain just then, but scrambled along as best I could. I kept on piping and piping and hobbling after the laddies until I could go no farther, and then seeing that the boys had won the position I began to get back as best I could to our own trenches.
>
> Quoted on www.webmatters.net/france/ww1_loos_2.htm

The men of the King's Own Scottish Borders advanced and despite heavy losses they reached the Germans' first-line trenches. Although wounded and eventually lying on the ground, Laidlaw kept playing his pipes and inspiring the advancing Borderers. Later he was awarded the Victoria Cross for his bravery.

Confusion and indecision

In many parts of the battlefield the Germans were pushed back. The Seaforth Highlanders, the Cameron Highlanders and the Black Watch all pushed into the German trenches but casualties were enormous. Reinforcements were needed and suddenly the attack plan fell apart.

General Haig was in charge of the attack but Sir John French, commander of the BEF, was in charge of reserve troops. He was reluctant to send in reserves made up of the mainly untried soldiers of Kitchener's New Army who were tired after a 40-mile long march in heavy rain. Meanwhile German reinforcements arrived and they repaired most of their damaged defences, including the barbed wire. After 24 hours of indecision and delay the British reinforcements were sent into battle but the British attack had lost the element of surprise, they had no gas cover and the Germans were waiting.

Slaughter

The German machine guns cut down the men from Kitchener's army in their thousands. Eventually the slaughter became so bad the German gunners stopped firing to allow the British to withdraw and take their wounded with them. A German diary recorded:

Source 2.12

Piper D. Laidlaw, V.C., Fr.C. de G. 7th KOSB. The legendary 'Piper of Loos' led the assault from the trenches, playing 'Blue Bonnets over the Border'.

> 66 *Ten columns of extended line in perfect alignment could clearly be distinguished, each one estimated at more than one thousand men, and offering such a target as had never been seen before, or even thought possible. Never had the machine-gunners such straightforward work to do nor done it so effectively. They moved their guns to and fro along the enemy's ranks unceasingly. The men stood on the fire-steps, some even on the parapets, and fired in glee into the mass of men advancing across open ground. As the entire field of fire was covered with the enemy's infantry the effect was devastating and they could be seen falling literally in hundreds.*

German diary entry for 25 September 1915

Source 2.13

Soldiers at the Battle of Loos in 1915

Loos was an 'almost win' with defeat snatched from the jaws of victory. Although the battle continued officially until 18 October 1915, in effect it finished after three days. Battalions from every Scottish regiment fought in the battle and the huge casualty figures meant that scarcely any part of the country was unaffected by the losses. For example, the 9th (Scottish) and 15th (Scottish) Divisions suffered 13,000 casualties. Some people described the battle as a meaningless and futile waste of lives. However, historian Sir John Keegan wrote how Scots 'seem to have shrugged off casualties and taken the setback only as a stimulus to renewed aggression.' (Quoted in Royle, *The Flowers of the Forest: Scotland and the Great War*, 2006, page 94).

Far from being demoralised and weakened by the slaughter, the Scots gained a huge reputation as feared and aggressive fighting troops. On 1 October 1915 Sir Henry Rawlinson said 'as a fighter, there is none to beat a Scotsman and a Highlander for preference'. As an example of that fighting spirit, Lieutenant Thorburn, 2nd Battalion Black Watch, reported seeing:

>
> *Another of our warriors had a German in each hand, gripping them by their chests, dragging them along and butting them in the face with his head, having apparently lost his rifle.*

Quoted in Derek Young, Scottish Voices from the Great War, 2005, page 139

One longer-term result of the failure at Loos was that Sir John French was replaced as commander by Douglas Haig, a Scot who would forever be associated with another battle on the Western Front – the Battle of the Somme.

The Battle of the Somme

The Battle of the Somme started on 1 July 1916. Three full Scottish divisions took part and many Scottish battalions also fought in other divisions. All of them had been told this was the 'Big Push' leading to victory. Once again hopes were to be destroyed.

For many months the German armies had been battering the French at Verdun. The British were under pressure to launch an attack to ease the strain on the French by diverting German forces to face the new attack. Sir William Robertson, Chief of the Imperial General Staff, explained why the attack on the Somme was launched:

Source 2.14

The man in charge of the Battle of the Somme was General Douglas Haig

>
> *The necessity of relieving pressure on the French Army at Verdun remains, and is more urgent than ever. This is, therefore, the first objective to be obtained by the combined British and French offensive. The second objective is to inflict as heavy losses as possible upon the German armies.*

Quoted on www.spartacus.schoolnet.co.uk/FWWsomme.html

The man in charge was General Douglas Haig who had replaced Sir John French at the end of 1915. Haig's view of the Western Front was straightforward: he believed that if he could gather together overwhelming firepower it could be used to destroy German defences and soldiers. He argued that defeating Germany would be inevitable if they could make the enemy fight and wear them down man by man, bullet by bullet. This was called a policy of attrition.

Haig planned to batter the enemy lines with an artillery barrage lasting seven days. Philip Gibbs, a journalist, described the final artillery barrage before the infantry went 'ower the bags':

> *It was a rolling thunder of shell fire, and the earth vomited flame, and the sky was alight with bursting shells. It seemed as though nothing could live, not an ant, under that stupendous artillery storm.*
>
> Quoted on www.spartacus.schoolnet.co.uk/FWWsomme.htm

Once the attack started Gibbs realised the artillery had not done its job well enough. He wrote:

> *There were conflicting reports as to the artillery's effectiveness and patrols sent out on the eve of the attack reported that the enemy front line was strongly held. Many of the rounds fired had been duds, while many others had been shrapnel which had little or no damaging effect on the enemy wire or trenches.*
>
> Quoted on www.spartacus.schoolnet.co.uk/FWWsomme.htm

In other words the enemy trenches were still well defended, many shells had failed to explode and the barbed wire had not been cut.

When the British attack began at 7.30a.m. the following day and the waves of men went over the top they were met by deadly machine-gun and mortar fire. Gibbs reported:

> *Our men got nowhere on the first day. They had been mown down like grass by German machine-gunners who, after our barrage had lifted, rushed out to meet our men in the open. Many of the best battalions were almost annihilated, and our casualties were terrible.*
>
> Quoted on www.spartacus.schoolnet.co.uk/FWWsomme.htm

Source 2.15

The attack on 1 July 1916 remains the worst day in the history of the British army.

The author John Buchan described the first day of the offensive at the Somme in his pamphlet, 'The Battle of the Somme (1916)':

The British moved forward in line after line, dressed as if on parade; not a man wavered or broke ranks; but minute by minute the ordered lines melted away under the deluge of high explosives, shrapnel, rifle, and machine-gun fire.

Quoted on www.spartacus.schoolnet.co.uk/FWWsomme.htm

On the first day of the battle the British suffered their highest ever casualties – almost 60,000 dead, wounded or missing. Official histories of the battle described how men fell in their ranks, mostly before the first hundred yards had been crossed. A lieutenant in the Seaforth Highlanders remembered:

I blew my whistle loud and clear and we clambered over the parapet into the open facing the German lines about 3–400 yards in front. Immediately there was an appalling din and we advanced under a hail of thousands of bullets whizzing through the air from rifles and machine guns, and with high explosive shells exploding and throwing up earth and metal, just Hell let loose.

Quoted in Derek Young, Scottish Voices from the Great War, 2005

Scots on the Western Front

What had gone wrong?

Many reasons have been put forward to explain the slaughter on the Somme. For some time the Germans had been strengthening their defences in the area, digging particularly deep concrete shelters. German machine gun teams therefore survived the initial bombardment and were ready to fire as troops advanced over no man's land. The bombardment itself had failed to knock out the German artillery and in many places the shells had failed to cut the German barbed wire. The attacking soldier's nightmare of advancing against barbed wire entanglements and withering machine-gun fire became reality – once again.

The Battle of the Somme has been described as the graveyard of Kitchener's armies and also of the various Pals' battalions. The 16th Battalion, the Highland Light Infantry, had been raised in Glasgow in 1914, mostly from past and present members of the Boy's Brigade. More than 500 ex-BBs from the battalion were killed on the Somme. These soldiers had joined in the wave of excitement in 1914. They came from the same streets of Glasgow and their deaths on the Somme devastated the close-knit communities back home. The same could be said for Cranston's and McCrae's Battalions of the Royal Scots, all from Edinburgh.

After two days the survivors of the first assault battalions had been moved back to the rear to recover and new battalions were sent out to carry on the attack. However, fresh attacks only added to the casualty lists. On 14 July a second phase of the battle started and the 51st Highland division alone lost 3500 men as they attacked High Wood. The first day of the new assault cost 9000 British lives.

The results

It seems incredible now to read the statement issued by the British Army on 3 July 1916 commenting on the Somme offensive:

 The first day of the offensive is very satisfactory. It is rather a slow, continuous, and methodical push, sparing in lives, until the day when the enemy's resistance, incessantly hammered at, will crumple up at some point.

Quoted on www.spartacus.schoolnet.co.uk/FWWsomme.htm

Despite the apparent callousness about lives lost, the last part of the statement holds some truth. Aware of the huge losses, Haig decided to push ahead with the plan but changed the objectives. Where once Haig believed the 'Big Push' could break the enemy lines to allow the cavalry to gallop through, he now accepted that a policy of attrition was most likely to win the war. When an Australian reporter asked Haig about the huge losses on the Somme Haig replied that it would be the side that showed the greatest fortitude (determination), regardless of losses, that would win the war.

After the war German commanders described the Battle of the Somme as 'the muddy grave of the German army'. In the long run the British army could replace its losses because the Empire and, by 1917, the USA stood behind Britain. But Germany had no allies ready to send fresh troops and no future hope of fresh resources. The Battle of the Somme was an expensive butcher's bill for both sides, but a bill that Britain could pay more easily than Germany.

Overall 400,000 British soldiers lost their lives on the Somme. Those who survived had lost the innocence of 1914. Scott MacFie of the Liverpool Scottish wrote to his father telling him that out of his company of 177 only 100 remained. He blamed the disaster on the Somme on a lack of preparation, vague orders, ignorance of objectives and 'horrid bungling'.

The battle had eased the pressure on the French at Verdun and it cost the Germans almost as many men as the British. But there had been no breakthrough and the battle faded away with the arrival of winter. Some would say the Somme was a win on points – but only just.

General Haig – bloody butcher or architect of victory?

The public stereotype of a Great War British General has been reinforced in many films and TV series, such as the character of General Melchett played by Stephen Fry in the TV series 'Blackadder goes Forth'. The General was insensitive to ever-increasing casualty figures, ignorant of the conditions fought in by his men, old fashioned and safely out of harms way in comfortable French châteaux. Some writers have described the British soldiers as 'lions led by donkeys' but the origin of this description pre-dates the Great War – 45 years earlier French forces fighting in the Franco–Prussian war in 1871 were described as 'lions led by pack asses'. The historical accuracy of the stereotype in relation to the Great War is questionable.

For most people Douglas Haig, commander of British forces on the Western Front from December 1915 until the end of the war, is the man most associated with the 'donkey' stereotype. Even today, many people still think of Haig as the Scot who caused the deaths of tens of thousands of his fellow countrymen. To others, however, Haig was the Scot who won the war for Britain.

Haig was born in Edinburgh into the wealthy Haig whisky family. In August 1914, when the war started, Haig was the General commanding the First Army Corps. On Christmas Day 1914 Haig was given command of First Army – the army he led at the Battle of Loos. The failure to break through at Loos and the argument over the control of reserves eventually led to Haig replacing Sir John French as Commander-in-Chief. Haig then remained as Commander of the BEF until the end of the war.

When Haig became Commander-in-Chief he was operating with explicit instructions from Kitchener to throw out the 'German Armies from French and Belgian territory', and to work closely with the French forces. The Western Front was already deadlocked when Haig became Commander and his new troops were untested and, in some cases, trained only to a very basic standard. Yet by 1918 Haig had broken the deadlock on the Western Front, turned a citizen army of raw recruits into an efficient war-winning force and fought and defeated the enemy in the main theatre of war. Complaints that he was an out-of-date cavalry officer seem out of place with his encouragement of tactics combining tanks, machine guns and aircraft.

Haig is often condemned as the General who sent hundreds of thousands of soldiers to their deaths at the Battle of the Somme. But did he have a choice? In 1916 he was under pressure from the British Government and the French to launch an attack. He argued for more time to prepare his new armies of volunteers but he was overruled.

Haig is also criticised for continuing the battle even when the horrific casualty figures became apparent. If Haig had called off the offensive on 2 July, what would have been gained? Lack of British co-operation would have angered the French and perhaps risked the alliance. As it was the Somme also cost many thousands of German lives and it can be argued that the attrition of the Somme was the beginning of the end for Germany. In 1940 John Buchan wrote:

 In the special circumstances of the campaign Haig's special qualities were the ones most needed – patience, sobriety, balance of temper, unshakeable fortitude [determination].

Quoted on www.spartacus.schoolnet.co.uk/FWWhaig.htm

What has been forgotten is that the Great War was a huge learning curve for all aspects of the military. In 1914 aircraft were barely able to carry any real weight and were held together with wire, struts and canvas. In the sodden trenches of 1914 soldiers were trying to cut fuses, insert them into hand grenades and then light them with matches all without being blown up themselves. The point is that the technology available to generals in 1918 simply was not there in 1914, or even 1915. New thinking, new armies and new technology, all under the direction of Haig, led to the victory of 1918.

It could be argued that the negative image of Haig dates from 1926, the year that the ex-Prime Minister Lloyd George published his memoirs. Lloyd George did not like Haig and it showed in the book, with Haig described as 'Brilliant to the top of his army boots.' The book also included statements by Haig taken out of context, such as 'The machine-gun is a much overrated weapon' and 'The nation must be taught to bear losses'. These statements helped to create a public impression of Haig as an insensitive, out of touch butcher responsible for hundreds of thousands of deaths on the Western Front. If that is true then how do we deal with the fact that it was Haig who turned thousands of ordinary civilians into an efficient modern army and led them to victory in 1918? Rather than be singled out as a 'bloody butcher', does Haig deserve to be remembered as the man who made victory possible – the architect of victory?

Critics of Haig who say that he 'won the war' only because the German army was exhausted and had to surrender fail to explain how that exhausted German army was able to inflict 380,000 casualties on the allied forces between August and November 1918. The German army did not fade away. They were defeated. In a letter to the *Times*, Monday 9 August 2008, this point was made:

 To devalue the capability that the British army developed during the Great War to learn from its experience, to adapt its operational tactics and to grind out its ultimate victory is to denigrate [lessen] the contribution of all those who participated, including Sir Douglas Haig.

The Times, Letters, 2008

The claim that Haig was insensitive to the losses sits uneasily with Haig's own words:

 No one can visit the Somme battlefield without being impressed with the magnitude of the effort of the British Army. To many it meant certain death, and all must have known that before they started. I have not the time to put down all the thoughts that rush into my mind when I think of all those fine fellows, who either have given up their lives for their country or have been maimed in its service. Later on I hope we may have a Prime Minister and a Government who will do them justice.

Quoted in Trevor Royle, The Flowers of the Forest: Scotland and the Great War, 2006

After the war Haig made great efforts to see justice was done to veterans. He was a central figure in the creation of the British Legion and the Earl Haig Fund, both of which were founded to help ex-servicemen. Cynics could claim that Haig was simply passing responsibility for the consequences of his actions on to other people and that in his charity work he was just trying to soothe his conscience – and so the debate goes on.

Activities

Teach a lesson

In groups of three or four, your task is to teach a lesson to the rest of your class which is linked to the theme of the Western Front.

You must deal with the following core points:

- Why did the Western Front develop?
- What were the main features of trench life?
- What were the main features of trench warfare?
- Why were the Battles of Loos and the Somme of such significance to Scotland?

Your main resource for information is this textbook but you must also research, find, beg or borrow other resources to make your lesson come alive. Think of the times you have been bored just listening to someone talk – your lesson must be different!

Negotiate with your teacher or tutor how long you have to prepare this lesson. It should be presented in an organised, interesting, mature and informative way. Planning is vital – and all members of your group must participate. It would be helpful to assign tasks such as a gopher to get items to be used in the lesson, a timekeeper to watch how your time is being used, a facilitator to keep things running smoothly in your group (they'll need tact and diplomacy!) and a recorder to note ideas and suggestions before you all forget them.

Negotiate the length of your lesson with your teacher or tutor. About 5 minutes would be appropriate. Remember, the lesson must have visual material – you could use Power Point or an overhead projector.

As in any lesson there are key things that you, as the teacher, must decide upon and aim for:

- What do you want your students to be able to do and know at the end of your lesson?
- How will you assess the success of your lesson? In other words what will you expect to see or hear your students doing to prove your lesson has been successful?

Activities

Poppy Day

'After the war Haig made great efforts himself to see justice was done to veterans. He was a central figure in the creation of the British Legion and the Earl Haig Fund, both of which were founded to help ex-servicemen.'

Either

It is November and you are selling red poppies as a symbol of remembrance. In the public mind in Scotland, these poppies are linked to the Earl Haig fund. Imagine you are confronted by someone who objects to what you are doing. They claim Haig was nothing but a butcher who did not care for his men. What arguments would you use to counter the objector?

Or

You are asked to wear a poppy in school but you refuse. What arguments linked to the Great War and the Haig poppy fund would you use when the head of your school asks for your reasons for refusal?

The Home Front – Scotland during the War 3

Voices against the war

Earlier in this book you read about the wave of patriotic war hysteria that swept over Britain in August 1914. What is not so well known is that there were people opposed to the war who did not wish to volunteer and who then resisted conscription.

Most people believe that when Kitchener launched his appeal for volunteers, men rushed to join up, never questioning the rights and wrongs of the war. That is not true. At the same time as Kitchener launched his appeal there were voices raised against the war. Soon after the war started 5000 people attended an anti-war demonstration held in Glasgow. Bertrand Russell, a pacifist who campaigned against the war, wrote on 15 August 1914:

 A month ago Europe was a peaceful group of nations: if an Englishman killed a German, he was hanged. Now, if an Englishman kills a German he is a patriot.

Quoted on www.spartacus.schoolnet.co.uk/

The strongest political group to oppose the war was the Independent Labour Party (ILP) which immediately attacked the official Labour Party's support for Kitchener's recruitment campaign. However, the ILP's newspaper, called *Forward*, was a lonely voice against the war when it published this anti-war message:

 If a man hints that there may be just something to be said for the other side, and that the whole war might someway have been avoided, he is at once set down as an unpatriotic, cranky, and absolutely impossible man.

Quoted in Catriona Macdonald and Elaine McFarland, Scotland and the Great War, *1998, page 64*

Anti-war opinion was not popular and the ILP was immediately criticised for being unpatriotic – perhaps understandable as the public was coming to terms with the reality of war. In the first two weeks of the war Britain suffered 20,000 casualties. One ILP member reminded others that their anti-war position would not gain support because:

> " With our hospitals filled with broken men, with bereaved families in every street ... in every village and hamlet, how can we expect people to listen to the arguments about the rights and wrongs of war? We must be tender and considerate to the feelings of our fellow workers, however hot our wrath against the war-makers.
>
> Quoted in Catriona Macdonald and Elaine McFarland, Scotland and the Great War, 1998, page 64

Source 3.1

Keir Hardie at an anti-war rally in London. There is no way of knowing how many in the crowd supported him.

Nevertheless, the ILP and other socialists continued to protest against the war. They argued that the war would be fought by ordinary working people whose lives, if they survived, would not change for the better. Why should a ship worker from Glasgow try to kill a ship worker from Bremen? Why should a crofter from Skye hate a farm labourer from Prussia?

By the end of 1914 ILP membership had fallen to 3000. Bruce Glazier, an ILP reporter from London visiting Scottish branches of the party, wrote in 1915:

> *The ILP is regarded with grave suspicion as a pacifist group, as a damper of the war enthusiasm of the nation, and a poisonous shrub in the glowing flowerbed of British patriotism.*
>
> *Quoted in Catriona Macdonald and Elaine McFarland,* Scotland and the Great War, *1998, page 67*

Nevertheless, Glazier also reported that in the Dundee, Leith and Glasgow branches of the party regular anti-war lectures and meetings were still being held.

Opposition to the war did not die and indeed it gained new life when conscription began in 1916.

Conscription

Conscription had been used to raise armies in other European countries for many years before the war. Young conscripts would spend about two years as soldiers in the army and then return to civilian life but remain on reserve, ready to be called back to the army if needed. In August 1914 these reservists were being called up to swell all of the armies of Europe with the exception of the British Army.

Even before war broke out parliament had debated the issue of conscription at least four times. Supporters of conscription argued that young men had a duty, above all else, to defend their country. When the voluntary recruitment rate seemed to fall after the initial rush in the late summer of 1914, the calls to introduce conscription became louder. As early as December 1914 the Glasgow Herald stated that if not enough volunteers joined up then conscription would be the only alternative. When it was reported that the recruitment rate had fallen from 300,000 each month in October 1914 to about 120,000 each month by early 1915, conscription seemed to be the inevitable next step.

War resisters had suspected all along that the introduction of conscription was only a matter of time. In January 1916 the Military Service Act brought in conscription for single men aged 19 to 40 years old. In May 1916 conscription was extended to include married men and by 1918 men up to the age of 50 were being conscripted. The Military Service Acts of 1916 made allowances for certain men to be exempt (excused) from military service. Men who were physically or mentally unfit were exempt and for all

Source 3.2

This socialist poster parodies recruitment posters. It suggests that those who profit from the war should face the reality of the conflict and not send the working classes to do their work for them.

> # To Arms!
>
> **Capitalists, Parsons, Politicians, Landlords, Newspaper Editors and Other Stay-At-Home Patriots.**
>
> ## your country needs
> # YOU
> ## in the trenches!!
>
> ### WORKERS
>
> ### Follow your Masters

others there were three categories of exemption. The first category exempted men involved in work of national importance to the war effort. For example, many coal miners were excused from military service. Another category exempted men if their service in the armed forces would cause 'serious hardship owing to his exceptional financial or business obligations or domestic position'. Finally, there was to be consideration for young men who refused to fight on grounds of their conscience. These 'conscientious objectors', or 'conchies' for short, claimed exemption on grounds of their political or religious beliefs.

In 1914 Clifford Allen and Fenner Brockway had started an organisation called the No Conscription Fellowship (NCF) in England. By early 1915 a Glasgow branch of the NCF had been formed. Later that same year the NCF spread across Scotland, while the ILP had started to compile its own registers of conscientious objectors. One report described Dundee as 'fair hotchin' with conscientious objectors. The NCF and ILP often mirrored each other's campaigns and were jointly condemned in the popular newspapers as cowards, peace cranks and 'pasty faces'. The NCF and ILP both opposed conscription and Fenner Brockway understood the socialist ILP position:

 The socialist conscientious objector has a group loyalty which is as powerful to him as the loyalty of the patriot for his nation. This group is composed of workers of all lands, the dispossessed, the victims of the present economic system, whether in peace or war.

Quoted on www.spartacus.schoolnet.co.uk/FWWpacifists.htm

Military tribunals judged whether or not to accept the claims of conscientious objection. Tribunals were made up of local people such as businessmen, landowners or shopkeepers and also one representative from the military. Clearly their intention was to conscript as many men as possible into the armed forces so appeals were often rejected. In Scotland it has been claimed that almost 70 per cent of all objectors were members of the ILP. Socialist James Maxton put forward a typical argument to his tribunal:

> 66 *I am a socialist and a member of a socialist organisation. As such I have worked to establish a better system of society, which would make for the peace and brotherhood of peoples of all lands. To take part in a war would be for me a desertion of these ideals, and I must therefore decline to take part.*

> *Quoted in Catriona Macdonald and Elaine McFarland,* Scotland and the Great War, *1998, page 71*

Source 3.3

A crowd of conscientious objectors to military service at a special prison camp.

Such an argument was unlikely to win exemption.

Across the UK 5970 'conchies' were court-martialled and sent to prison. Conditions were harsh but a former Home Secretary Sir George Cave had claimed that conscientious objectors preferred the 'quiet safety of prison' to the dangers of the trenches. In response, peace campaigners pointed out that soldiers who were in prison for serious crimes almost always asked to be returned to the front line to escape the horror of what they had to face in prison. At least 73 conscientious objectors died because of the harsh treatment they received.

In total, about 16,000 men from across the UK refused to fight. Most of these men were pacifists who believed that it was wrong to kill another human being.

'Conchies' were given choices to make. Around 7000 conscientious objectors agreed to perform non-combat duties, often as stretcher-bearers in the front-line, but more than 1500 pacifists refused all military service. They argued that by performing a non-combat role in the war effort they would be releasing other soldiers into combat roles and therefore they would be fighting 'by proxy'. These 'absolutists' opposed undertaking any work whatsoever that helped Britain's war effort.

There were also 'alternativists' who were prepared to take on civilian work but not supervised by the military. Many Scottish socialists took this option rather than go to prison, arguing that their message would not be heard from inside prison. James Maxton explained:

> *I appreciated and understood the attitude of my friends who absolutely declined to do anything, and suffer continuous imprisonment over the whole war period, but it did not suit my philosophy, which demanded active carrying on of the class struggle, nor did it suit my temperament to be confined when the urge within me was to be out trying to influence my fellows to use the opportunities presented by war conditions for the purpose of social revolution.*
>
> *Quoted in Catriona Macdonald and Elaine McFarland,* Scotland and the Great War, *1998, page 73*

Religious groups and churches were divided over the issue of conscientious objectors. The big church groups supported the war effort and the Very Reverend Sir George Adam Smith attacked conscientious objectors in his opening address as Moderator of the Church of Scotland. It was difficult for individual church leaders to speak out in parishes that were suffering the losses of their young men but Rev. Malcolm McCallum warned: 'beware, for this war was neither God's war not a Holy War! It was a war of sinful men between misguided brothers!' (Quoted in Macdonald and McFarland, *Scotland and the Great War*, 1998, page 68) Religious representatives were present at military tribunals and on one occasion a conscientious objection on religious grounds that 'Christ told us to love our enemies' was rejected with the response 'we can love our enemies and kill them at the same time'.

When the war ended the issue of the increase in power of the state over its citizens was far from over. In particular, the ILP campaigned for the repeal

The Home Front – Scotland during the War

of the Military Service Act. On 11 April 1919 a large crowd gathered at the St Andrews Halls, Glasgow, to hear various speakers call for 'the abolition of conscription and the release of all conscientious objectors'. Thirteen hundred conscientious objectors were still in prison five months after armistice, though it should be noted that the war did not officially end until June 1919, when Germany was declared no longer a threat.

In May 1919 the longest-serving conscientious objectors began to be released and by August there were no more 'conchies' imprisoned. Often they returned to civilian life to find that their families shunned them, employers refused to offer jobs and parliament tried to deny those who had refused non-combatant service the right to vote for five years.

Throughout the war the ILP had remained consistently opposed to the conflict. Although it was heavily criticised in the early months of the war, by 1918 many thousands of ordinary Scots had listened to the ILP's anti-war message. The ILP could reasonably claim 'the ILP in Scotland lives, and in 201 towns and villages bears witness to the vitality of the socialist movement.' (Quoted in Macdonald and McFarland, *Scotland and the Great War*, 1998, page 77).

ILP branches had grown from 112 to 167 and membership had swollen from just under 3000 to 9000. Branches of the ILP had taken root in Inverurie, Buckie, Keith and Craigellachie. It was even reported 'the ILP is in Banffshire!' On the other hand, it is important to remember that compared with the millions who were directly involved in the war effort, the pacifists and war resisters were a tiny group of people, calculated at less than half of one percent of the population. Compulsory military conscription was finally abolished in December 1920.

Activities

You are working for the government in the autumn of 1915 and have been asked to prepare a report recommending whether or not the government should introduce conscription.

You must use extensive background knowledge in your report. The report should:

- recommend whether or not conscription should be introduced
- provide arguments to support your conclusions
- identify and comment on any arguments which may be presented by those who oppose your recommendation.

You may be required to present your report in a written form or as a spoken presentation lasting between 2 and 4 minutes.

The changing role of women

The Great War is often seen as a major turning point in the role of women in British society. The usual image is of women doing men's work, keeping the country running smoothly during the war and being rewarded for their efforts by being given the right to vote in 1918. To an extent this image is true. The war opened up jobs to women that would otherwise have been closed to them and in 1918 some women were given the right to vote in national elections. Only a few years earlier newspaper headlines had reported women on hunger strikes and being force fed as the government struggled with campaigners for the female right to vote. However, the question of how far the war caused a complete change in male attitudes towards women is open to debate.

Changes before 1914

Before the war it was widely believed that a woman's place was in the home but there were signs that attitudes were changing before 1914. Some women gained access to better education and also to some jobs in the professions. New laws had improved the legal rights of women. The overall effect of these developments was to erode male prejudices but women still had no vote and without that, it was argued, they had no political leverage to force further changes. Women who campaigned for the right to vote argued that only by winning the vote could they significantly improve their lives and status in society.

In 1897 several local women's suffrage societies united to form the National Union of Women's Suffrage Societies (NUWSS) which believed in moderate, 'peaceful' tactics to win the vote, mainly for

Source 3.4

Not all suffragette tactics were violent. These Dundee suffragettes relied on handing out leaflets and booklets to get their message across.

middle-class property-owning women. Later, the NUWSS was nicknamed the Suffragists, in contrast to the later Suffragettes – the popular name for the Women's Social and Political Union (WSPU). The WSPU was formed in 1903 by Emmeline Pankhurst who was frustrated by the lack of progress achieved by the NUWSS. At first the suffragettes demonstrated peacefully with rallies and processions but by 1910 the suffragette campaign turned to more violent tactics. As a result more and more suffragettes were arrested and by the summer of 1914 over 1000 suffragettes were in prison.

Britain declared war on Germany in August 1914 and two days later the NUWSS suspended its political campaigning for the vote. To encourage the suffragettes to end their campaign the government agreed to release all WSPU prisoners if the suffragette protests ended. With a grant of over £2000 from the government, a WSPU pro-war propaganda campaign encouraged men to join the armed forces and women to demand 'the right to serve' with slogans such as 'For Men Must Fight and Women Must work'. The WSPU even changed the name of their newspaper from *The Suffragette* to *Britannia*.

During the Great War women found themselves in locations and jobs unexpected by them or anyone else before 1914. As casualty rates increased on the battlefield and conscription was introduced to swell the ranks, women were needed to fill the gaps on the Home Front. Industries that had previously excluded women now welcomed them. Women worked as conductors on trams and buses, as typists and secretaries and nearly 200,000 women found work in government departments. Thousands worked on farms, at the docks and even in the police.

Source 3.5

Mairi Chisholm was only 18 when she went to the front line as a volunteer nurse.

Many other women used their nursing skills to help the wounded and some women were more determined than others to get as close to the front line as possible. One such person was Mairi Chisholm.

In August 1914, 18-year-old Mairi Chisholm left her home in Scotland and rode her motor bike to London looking for war work. She was seen riding at speed through the streets of London by Dr Hector Munro, who was then organising a medical team to go to Belgium. Chisholm explained why she went:

> *The Belgians had not expected war and their medical arrangements were mixed and obviously their men were in a terrible state and so it was a rescue affair and a great emergency.*
>
> The Chisholm Papers

When they arrived in Belgium, Chisholm discovered that only one in six casualties survived the journey to hospital. As a result Munro and his team proposed setting up a first aid post immediately behind the front line. The Belgian authorities agreed but expected the nurses to give up after 24 hours. Instead, the nurses worked constantly for the next 18 months. Chisholm wrote in her dairy:

> *Forty eight hours on duty at a stretch with about 500 dead or dying or wounded soldiers to attend to have often constituted what I might term a day's work for us in the first stages of the war.*
>
> The Chisholm Papers

By working so close to the front line the women were in constant danger. Chisholm wrote:

> *The German shells are falling quite close and it is like hell itself – one's head is splitting with the din. The German fire is working up this way and now one can see the German shells bursting about a mile away. I wonder how long I shall have to remain here in the midst of this.*
>
> The Chisholm Papers

Chisholm and the other nurses became famous for their exploits and care for the wounded.

> *We worked a lot to rescue pilots who had been shot down in no man's land. We used to have to make expeditions to try and get the pilots out. We went on foot, not always with stretchers, just hoping to be able to get them with their arms around our necks.*
>
> The Chisholm Papers

Chisholm's nursing bravery was rewarded in January 1915 when the King of the Belgians awarded her the Order of Leopold. She wrote of her delight:

> 66 *I could hardly believe it. To be made a Knight and to receive the highest medal honour of all, the equivalent of our Victoria Cross, was wonderful.*
>
> The Chisholm Papers

In March 1918 Chisholm and the other nurses were gassed and although Chisholm recovered and returned to post she was not fully fit. Her adventure came to an end in March 1918:

> 66 *Three and a half years of being privileged to work in danger alongside brave men. The cause was greater than ourselves.*
>
> The Chisholm Papers

Source 3.6

When a Russian official saw Elsie Inglis working he said 'No wonder England is a great country if the women are like that.' He must have meant it was Scots that made England great!

Perhaps more famously, Elsie Inglis was another Scot who combined her early feminism with her medical skills to assist in the war effort.

Elsie Inglis studied medicine at the Edinburgh School of Medicine for Women, the Edinburgh Medical College and also trained at the Glasgow Royal Infirmary. She was also a member of the NUWSS and played an important role in setting up the Scottish Women's Suffrage Federation but it was the Great War that made her widely known.

Inglis was the driving force in the creation of the Scottish Women's Hospitals Committee that sent over 1000 women doctors, nurses, orderlies and drivers to war zones across Europe and the Balkans. Inglis was also involved in setting up four Scottish Women's Hospitals, which had much lower levels of death from disease than the more traditional military hospitals.

Having endured terrible conditions, capture, repatriation and also fighting against male-dominated decision-making in the UK, Elsie Inglis eventually died from cancer in November 1917.

Dilution

By 1916 it was clear that women had become a vital part of the war effort, so much so that the *Glasgow Herald* reported in early 1916: 'The women are magnificent and the nation is indebted to them'. The biggest increase in female employment was in the previously male-dominated engineering industry. Over 30,000 women were employed during the war making munitions in Scotland, whereas just before the war less than 4000 women worked in heavy industry in Scotland.

At first trade unions were concerned over the issue of dilution. A skilled male worker had to serve an apprenticeship of seven years. That skilled man could then demand a wage reflecting his skill. In contrast, women spent only a few weeks in training to do the same skilled jobs and unions and their members were worried that the higher wages of men would be at risk after the war, or that the skilled men be replaced by less well-paid women workers. As the demand for more and more weapons and munitions grew, the need to find an answer to the dilution row became urgent.

Source 3.7

Skilled engineers were always men before the war. They were worried about losing their jobs and their status if women could do their work!

The Ministry of Munitions introduced a dilution scheme whereby skilled jobs were broken down into individual processes. A woman could then be trained in that process and was allowed to work while under supervision. That way many women could be trained in different processes so the job was done but the status and skill of the 'skilled man' was not undermined. The Munitions of War Act of 1915 also suggested that women should be paid comparable rates to men but employers soon found ways of avoiding that commitment. In Scotland the main munitions centres were in Glasgow, Clydebank and Gretna, the latter becoming the first 'new town' planned by the government to house 9000 women workers and 5000 men.

The munitions factories were dangerous and unpleasant, with women working around the clock with explosive mixtures described as the 'devil's porridge'. In total, 61 workers died from poisoning and 71 from explosions.

The rent strikes of 1915

The rent strikes of 1915, mainly in and around Glasgow, seem far removed from the work of nurses such as Mairi Chisholm and the munitions workers at Gretna. However, there is a connection – all three are examples of how women responded to the challenge of life during the Great War.

The rent strikes of 1915 are significant for several reasons but mainly because they showed how ordinary people, especially women, could organise themselves to take on authority and improve their own living conditions.

By 1915 Glasgow and the industrial west of Scotland faced a huge increase in population as war workers arrived looking for a place to live. The bulk of houses in Glasgow were tenement blocks and many of these had very poor living conditions. The condition of the buildings was made worse by a lack of tradesmen who were otherwise involved in the war effort. Landlords took little notice of the difficulties. Workers searching for accommodation took what they could get and with demand rising landlords simply increased rents. In Govan, for example, rents increased by around 20 per cent. Those with money paid high prices for a poor quality home; those who could not pay were evicted. It appeared also that landlords took advantage of so many men being away in the armed forces and bullied the women left behind with threats of eviction if they did not pay up. With rising food prices and rents taking a large part of weekly earnings, the protests increased. The women of Glasgow had had enough!

Source 3.8

'We want Justice.' The posters make a big point about the unfairness of women and children being exploited while their men are away fighting for their country.

In February 1915 Helen Crawfurd, Mary Barbour, Agnes Dollan and Jessie Stephens helped to form the Glasgow Women's Housing Association to resist the rent rises and threatened evictions

The tactics of the women were simple – make it impossible for the authorities to evict tenants by blocking access to the tenements by crowding into the stair closes and 'bombing' sheriff officers with bags of flour.

Although it might seem the rent strikes were a local concern the issues raised by the strikes had national importance. Glasgow and the Clyde area were vital to the war effort, especially the munitions industry, and any possible disruption to production worried the government. The women therefore made a big point of arguing that they were not disrupting the war effort. Instead, they argued that fair rents would prevent landlords profiteering and exploiting the incoming war munitions workers and also prevent local workers from being evicted for non payment of unfair rents.

Source 3.9

How useful is this poster as evidence that the rent strikes politicised women?

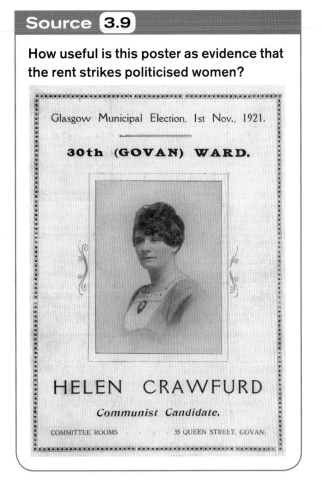

Glasgow Municipal Election, 1st Nov., 1921.

30th (GOVAN) WARD.

HELEN CRAWFURD

Communist Candidate.

COMMITTEE ROOMS - - - 35 QUEEN STREET, GOVAN.

Source 3.10

Notice how the rent strikers linked the landlords with the Germans in the public mind. In reality there was no connection but mud sticks!

The women's campaign entered a new phase when landlords started to threaten the protestors with eviction, fines or prison. In retaliation the women began a rent strike in May 1915. Soon about 25,000 tenants in Glasgow had joined the strike with other strikes starting to take root in Aberdeen and Dundee.

The campaign escalated when munitions workers joined the strike and were taken to court. Outside the court protestors carried banners declaring 'We are fighting the Huns at Home' and 'Fighting Prussians in Partick'. Even the employers supported the protestors, fearing that court disputes would slow their production by taking workers away. Fairfields engineering works even stated they would not allow any of their workers to move into the house of an evicted person.

By November the protests had grown even more. A mass demonstration in Glasgow's George Square was held on 17 November to protest against the prosecution of eighteen tenants for non payment of rent increases. The atmosphere of protest and discontent worried the government. Men were now striking in war munitions and engineering factories in protest against the actions of the landlords and to agitate for pay increases of their own.

Eventually a solution was found in the Rent Restriction Act, a new law that froze rents at 1914 levels unless improvements had been made to the property. The rent strikes had been provoked by a sense of outrage that landlords were taking advantage of a situation to make profit at a time when the country was fighting to win a war. David Kirkwood, a socialist campaigner within the ILP, wrote: 'if the nation is to have an adequate supply of munitions of war, the workers must have healthy housing accommodation.' (Quoted in Royle, *The Flowers of the Forest: Scotland and the Great War*, 2006, page 190) The strikers demands had been met, protests and profiteering now declined and wartime production was maintained without disruption.

The vote at last

Having seen the various ways that women contributed to the war effort it has become something of a cliché to suggest that women gained the right to vote as a thank you for their efforts in the war. How far can that view be supported? Did women's valuable work for the war effort radically change male ideas about their role in society? Or is that view over simplistic, overlooking the pre-1914 changes of attitude and ignoring certain important points. After the war, for example, women were ejected from the 'men's work' they had done during the war years and in government policy and advertising the idea that a woman's place was in the home was as strong as it had ever been. Also remember that the women who worked long hours and risked their lives in munitions factories were mostly single, in their late teens or early 20s – the women who were given the vote in 1918 were 'respectable' ladies, aged 30 or over.

Perhaps a more realistic answer is that the government saw an advantage in further franchise reform, part of which was extending the vote to women. The Russian Revolution had made governments across Europe worried of any social disorder. Rent strikes and industrial unrest in Glasgow and the west of Scotland had led eventually to tanks and soldiers in the streets of Glasgow. Could the government risk more protest and disorder after the war? Such fears were not unrealistic, given that women who had done such valuable work during the war were facing redundancy or being pressured into returning to 'women's work'. Could the government be sure that these women would not join a new suffragette campaign after the war and return to suffragette 'terrorism'?

Was political reform inevitable by 1918?

The relationship between male UK citizens and their government had changed. When conscription was introduced in 1916 men were ordered to join the armed forces or do work of national importance. Was it right that the government could order men to fight and kill on its behalf and not allow these men a chance to choose the government? Politicians also grew anxious to enfranchise more men, many of whom had lost their qualification as a result of moving home for war service. It was politically unacceptable to tell those ex-soldiers that they had lost their right to vote and so the rules had to change. With franchise reform inevitable it was seen as an opportunity to defuse the potential problem of militant female protest after the war by giving the vote to some women while change was in the air anyway.

If you combine those arguments with the sight of women 'doing their bit' for the war effort and eroding the negative publicity of the earlier suffragette campaign it can be seen why the time for votes for women had arrived.

The 1918 Representation of the People Act gave women over the age of 30 who were householders, the wives of householders, occupiers of property with an annual rent of £5 or graduates of British universities the right to vote in national elections. It also gave all men over the age of 21 the right to vote (and aged 19 if they had been on active service in the armed forces). The electorate increased to about 21 million, of which 8.4 million were women – about 40 per cent of the total voters.

Had the war really changed the role of women?

In political terms, many women could now vote and by the end of the 1920s women had voting equality with men. In social terms little had changed for women. Some former suffragettes transferred their campaigning to better conditions for working mothers, such as access to child care facilities, but the wartime change had been a temporary one. The majority of women did not keep their wartime jobs when the war ended. The Restoration of Pre-War Practices Act meant that returning soldiers were given back their jobs and with the closure of most munitions factories women workers were no longer needed. Within a few years of the end of the war over 25 per cent of

all working women were back in domestic service – child minding and house work. That total was more than before the war. The economic slump of the 1920s was the final blow to the hopes of women for a continuation of the opportunities opened up by the Great War. While 'respectable' women over 30 got the vote most other women just returned to life as it had been before the war.

Activities

Women at war

Work in pairs or groups of three.

Design **three** wordsearches, each one no larger than 10 squares by 10 squares.

- One of your puzzles must contain only words or phrases linked to the main themes or issues in this chapter, e.g. dilution, rent strikes.
- Your second puzzle must contain only words or phrases linked to the actions of the government or the protesters.
- Your third puzzle must contain only names of significant people in this chapter.

The words or phrases can go in any direction and phrases can be split.

Each word or phrase must have a definition or clue to help someone find it.

When you have completed your puzzles, exchange them with another group or person and find the answers to the puzzles you receive.

DORA

The Defence of the Realm Act (known as DORA) became law on 8 August 1914.

'Realm' is an old word for kingdom or country, so DORA gave the government wide-ranging emergency powers to take action for the safety and security of the whole of the UK during the war. More new laws followed to define more clearly the powers of the government under DORA. For example, on 27 November 1914 an Act to consolidate and amend the Defence of the Realm Acts stated:

>
> *Be it enacted by the King's most Excellent Majesty, by and with the advice and consent of the Parliament, as follows:*
>
> *The government has power during the continuance of the present war to issue regulations for securing the public safety and defence of the realm, designed:*
>
> *(a)* *to prevent persons communicating with the enemy or obtaining information for that purpose or any purpose calculated to jeopardise [endanger] the success of the operations of any of His Majesty's forces or the forces of his allies or to assist the enemy; or*
>
> *(b)* *to secure the safety of His Majesty's forces and ships and the safety of any means of communication and of railways, ports, and harbours; or*
>
> *(c)* *to prevent the spread of false reports or reports likely to interfere with the success of His Majesty's forces by land or sea.*
>
> *Quoted on www.nationalarchives.gov.uk/pathways/ firstworldwar/transcripts/first_world_war/defence_ofthe-realm*

When war broke out the government was concerned at first with protecting the country's ports and railways from sabotage, controlling resources and communications and defending against spies. The public was warned to be on the look out for any suspicious persons, no matter how unlikely the situation.

DORA also increased control over what people could know about the war. In August 1914 the British government established the War Office Press Bureau. Reports of the fighting were limited and in the early months of the war reporters were not allowed anywhere near the fighting. News was censored and even letters home from soldiers were first passed through a military censor. Even when restrictions were relaxed, news reporters were still under strict control about what could or could not be published. Supporters of DORA could easily argue that news of any casualties or details of military action might help the enemy but sometimes the 'official news' did not match the reality of the casualty figures. For example, Source 3.11 suggests the attack on the Somme had been a huge success. The reality was somewhat different.

Source 3.11

What was better to give the public – a smiling Tommy having beaten the Germans, or news of 60,000 dead, wounded and missing on Day 1 of the attack?

WELL DONE, THE NEW ARMY!

In 1915 there was a munitions crisis because private companies were unable to produce enough munitions – partly because the companies were too small and partly because they could not get enough metal, coal, rubber and other materials. Under the terms of DORA, the government took control of co-ordinating the supply of materials. It also set up its own munitions factories and took control of the coal industry in 1917.

DORA also allowed the government to set the opening and closing times of pubs. Before the war pubs could stay open for 13 hours each day, apart from Sundays, and there was no limit on what could be drunk. By 1916 opening hours had been gradually reduced so that eventually pubs were only open for five and a half hours per day, closing at 9p.m., with no Sunday opening. It was also alleged that DORA was responsible for stopping the buying of rounds, called 'treating', and for weakening the strength of beer. What is true is that restrictions on alcohol were most strictly enforced near munitions factories – war-time production had to be kept high! Lloyd George made few friends when he blamed problems in munitions production on the heavy drinking habits of workers in the west of Scotland, rather than the inefficiency of the factories or management.

DORA, the Highlands and the land question

As the war went on and food supplies in Britain became more of a concern DORA was used to maximise food production within the country. As part of DORA local councils could take over land that was not being used for food production and grow crops on it. Propaganda to eat less and grow more spread across the country but in the Highlands DORA, food production and the old issue of land ownership and possible land seizures became interlinked.

In practical terms the only people who were readily available to farm local land were the local crofters. Pre-war legislation about high compensation to deer forest landlords had proved unworkable during the war and faced with threats to seize land officials used the DORA arrangements to head off conflict. It seemed a practical solution to the needs of the war effort but beneath the surface the old tensions over land ownership still rumbled on. By allowing the local crofting tenants temporary access to land the authorities were hoping to avoid land seizures erupting again. The tenancy agreements were to last for three years, ending like other DORA arrangements with the end of the war. After the war a return to pre-war arrangements was not always possible as some tenants refused to return the land to the previous owners. That difficulty and the whole issue of the post-war land question in the Highlands are dealt with in a later chapter.

Opposition to DORA

As government powers increased, so did criticism of DORA. On one level people complained of the apparent pettiness of DORA and a cartoon of the time showed DORA as a miserable old woman determined to make Britain a joyless place. While it was good sense to stop people photographing military bases, it was less obvious why flagpoles were banned or why permits were needed to keep homing pigeons. In the last two cases the government was concerned about signals or messages being sent to the enemy. However, on a more serious level criticism of DORA centred around the destruction of Britain's liberal traditions and what would today be called civil liberties.

The political idea of liberalism, certainly before 1914, was that there should be as little government interference in the lives of citizens as possible. The war changed that outlook as government took over control of so much of daily life. In another part of this book you will read how the once-strong Liberal party became much less important after the war. One reason for that was the change in attitudes about government involvement in people's lives and the move away from liberalism as an ideology. Critics of DORA felt the government was abusing its powers and silencing legitimate political debate, including anti-war opinion. Laws which gave the government complete power to suppress criticism being published and imprison without trial went directly against the civil liberties that had been gained in Britain over a long time. DORA also gave military authorities the power to try people by courts martial – a restriction of civil liberty because alleged wrong-doers were tried by a jury of army officers, not civilians.

Politically, DORA was used to prevent criticism of the war effort, especially in newspaper reports. Such anti-war or anti-government messages were most often found in the left-wing socialist newspapers. When criticised the government could always fall back on the excuse that what they did was for the war effort. Anyone who criticised the government was accused of undermining the war effort and of being unpatriotic. At the time of the tensions associated with Red Clydeside in 1915, the ILP newspaper, *Forward*, was closed for some months, as was another left-wing paper called *Vanguard*.

Socialists and members of the ILP were the main opposition to DORA. In the article that caused *Forward* to be shut down John Maclean had written:

> Unless the Clyde men act quickly, determinedly, and with a clear object in view they are going to be tied in a knot. We know that the Glasgow press was threatened with the Defence of the Realm Act should it make mention of strike had one broken out.

Quoted in Trevor Royle, The Flowers of the Forest: Scotland and the Great War, 2006, pages 234–5

Maclean argued against the increasing power of the state and many others shared his concern. William Scott, Professor of Political Economy at Glasgow University, believed 'the freedom of the individual must be absorbed into the national effort for a time but it is to be hoped only for a time'. Maclean was arrested under the Defence of the Realm Act 1915 for his anti-government and left-wing opinions. He was found guilty of making statements likely to undermine recruiting. Maclean experienced several spells in prison and by 1918 he was physically and mentally weakened by his treatment under DORA.

Criticism of DORA also increased when conscription was introduced. The issue of conscription is dealt with elsewhere in this book but it should not be forgotten that conscription had not been used in Britain before and its introduction was seen by some people as yet another increase in the power of the state at the cost of individual liberty. Liberal MP Richard Lambert summed up the issue when he argued that the roots of British liberty lay in the free services of a free people. Conscription took away the spirit of voluntary service which, Lambert argued, lay at the heart of Liberalism and British freedoms.

Conscription did not just apply to men being taken into the armed forces. Men could be conscripted to work in jobs of national importance. The main difference was that conscripted workers were no longer civilians. They were under military authority and discipline. That authority would deny them the right to strike, thereby ensuring supplies remained unthreatened. That point was not lost on left-wing supporters and John Maclean wrote:

 We know that the military authorities had engineers and other workers in the army ready to draft into the Clyde works in the event of a strike. We know also that, despite clamour for munitions, young men are being dismissed from all the Clyde works in order to force them into the army. When the occasion arises they will be reinstated in their old jobs, but now as military slaves. Quick and firm action is needed if slavery is going to be abolished and conscription defeated.

Quoted in Trevor Royle, The Flowers of the Forest: Scotland and the Great War, 2006, page 235

Although Maclean had many supporters on the Clyde, the government had overwhelming public support for its actions. The public believed government action was necessary to win the war even if, as one commentator put it, the country had to become more like Prussia to defeat Prussianism. The public and the press had earlier criticised the government for not doing enough to win the war so they were not now going to complain about the erosion of civil liberties or worry about people protesting about government restrictions of their freedom.

Commemoration and Remembrance

On 11 November 1918 an armistice ended the conflict that was known as the Great War. News of the armistice was greeted with celebration in some areas, relief in others and everywhere with memories of loved ones who would never be seen again.

According to some newspaper reports, Armistice Day was the greatest day of rejoicing Glasgow has ever known but for most people the news was tinged with sadness. Few families in Scotland escaped the loss of a father, son, brother, husband, boyfriend, neighbour or friend. In many places people accepted the news with quiet thoughts and some sadness. The *Shetland Times* reported 'there were no indications of hilarity. The strain had been too great, the tensions too strong to permit levity [fun and laughter]'. (Quoted in Royle, *The Flowers of the Forest: Scotland and the Great War*, 2006, page 278) Thousands of Scots grieved for their friends and, perhaps, for a Scotland that would never return.

Taking the war as a whole, it has been calculated that over 5,500 people had been killed every single day for 1564 days – the length of the war. None of the Scottish regiments that fought in the war escaped high casualties.

The Royal Scots suffered casualties before they even reached the front line: 217 men, mostly from the Leith area, were killed in a railway disaster near Gretna in May 1915. When they arrived at Gallipoli to fight Germany's ally Turkey, they had a 40 per cent casualty rate for no obvious gains.

During the retreat from Mons in autumn 1914 the Royal Scots Fusiliers had only 70 men left out of 1000. At Loos, the 15th (Scottish) Division lost many men in the opening minutes when their own gas blew back in their faces. At Nueve Chappelle the 2nd Cameronians lost 70 per cent of its men in an attack on German positions across open ground.

Source 3.12

Coldstream War Memorial – like thousands of others across the land these memorials provided a focus for grief and respect. They continue to do so almost a hundred years later.

On the first day of the Somme the 2nd Seaforth Highlanders lost 500 men. The Gordon Highlanders and the Argyll and Sutherland Highlanders both had similar losses. Over the course of the war the Royal Scots lost 11,000 men. The Gordon Highlanders lost 9,000 and the Black Watch suffered the most of the Highland regiments with 10,000 dead. Glasgow lost 18,000 of its young men, Dundee lost 4000 and Lewis suffered one of the highest casualty rates in the UK, with the loss of 17 per cent of the Lewismen who served in the armed forces. After four years of propaganda justifying Britain's part in the war, attacking the enemy and promising a better future, the Scottish population needed confirmation that their losses had not been in vain.

Remembering the dead

The exact number of Scottish war dead will probably never be known. The official figure given at the end of the war was 74,000 but others argue that it was more. 'A hundred thousand dead' became a rallying cry for those campaigning for a national Scottish war memorial. Later still, a higher figure of almost 150,000 was calculated by including Scots from around the world 'killed in the service of the crown' – but was a Scot killed while serving in the Australian forces counted as a Scottish casualty or an Australian? Other difficulties arose when trying to calculate those who died as a result of wounds received in the war or because of their experiences in the war. The point is that the exact figure does not really matter. Each and every casualty of the war was a person loved by someone whose life was darkened forever when the news came of that individual's death. On living room walls across the country were scrolls and medals sent by the government.

However, there was also a need for a more collective, public recognition of the nation's loss. Even before the war ended discussions had started about how best to remember the war dead. In 1917 a decision was made to create a UK memorial in London and a museum to show the part played by the armed forces in the war. These places became known as the Cenotaph and the Imperial War Museum respectively. Scotland supported both London-based projects but there was also a feeling that Scotland should remember its own sons and daughters in some way. The Duke of Atholl summed up the feeling when he said the Scottish nation would put up a memorial 'with their own hands in their own country and with their own money'.

Source 3.13

The scroll sent to families of military personnel killed in action during the First World War.

Fairly soon afterwards, a decision was reached that the most appropriate location would be Edinburgh Castle and the famous architect Sir Robert Lorimer was commissioned to start work on the design. Then the

arguments started. The estimated cost of Lorimer's design was £250,000 (about £10 million today). As well as concerns over the cost, there were also protests about the damage that would be done to the distinctive skyline of Edinburgh Castle and that the planned building in some way glorified war. Even a former prime minister, the Earl of Rosebury, compared the design to 'a huge jelly mould'. By 1922 criticism had grown so fierce that a full-sized model of the planned building was put up in the castle! A revised design was created and eventually the memorial was officially opened on 14 July 1927.

Source 3.14

An early photograph of the Scottish National War memorial. Notice the rows of poppy wreaths.

At the opening service crowds thronged the castle esplanade as the rolls of honour for each of Scotland's regiments were placed in Scotland's National Memorial, described by writer Ian Hay as 'a coronach [or funeral lament] in stone'. For thousands of Scottish families whose loved ones were never found or were buried in far away places, the national memorial became a place of pilgrimage. Every year tens of thousands of fingers still trace over the names of their loved ones in the registers of the dead in a search for comfort and meaning.

The national memorial built within Edinburgh Castle marked the nation's grief and loss but communities needed to claim their 'ain folk'. In the years that followed the Great War smaller but no less important memorials were put up in towns and villages across Scotland in order to remember and

commemorate community loss. These memorials can be seen today in the smallest of villages and in the largest cities. Sometimes the act of remembrance looked to the future, as at Stenton, East Lothian, where the village hall was built to benefit future generations. In the tiny village of Fogo, near Duns in the Scottish Borders, a lych gate was built over the seventeenth-century kirkyard entrance with the names of the war dead clearly seen.

Source 3.15

The lych gate at Fogo Kirkyard

All of these memorials had a common hope – that the dead had not died in vain and that the Great War really would be the war to end all wars. By 1945, at the end of the Second World War, disillusionment had set in. There are very few memorials dedicated only to the dead of the Second World War – in most cases the later names were added to the memorials of the Great War.

Many families had to cope with the knowledge that their loved ones had been obliterated by the war or were buried overseas. They had no body to bury or place to grieve. In an attempt to provide a last resting place and a focus for grieving families the Imperial War Graves Commission created and cared for military cemeteries around the world. Each grave had a headstone recording the soldier's name, rank, regiment and date of death. For those unidentified bodies the inscription reads 'a soldier of the Great War, known only to God'. These cemeteries, over 600 of them in France and Flanders in Belgium, also became places of pilgrimage for Scottish families in the 1920s and to the present day.

Activities

Remembrance

The year is 1922 – four years since the fighting stopped. Your town is dedicating its new war memorial. How do you feel about the new memorial?

Explain your thoughts as if you were:

an ex-soldier who had volunteered in 1914

OR

a widow whose husband and two sons were killed in the war

OR

a member of the ILP who served time in prison as a conscientious objector.

4 Scotland at Work and at War

The impact of the war on Scottish industry and the economy

In 1914 Scottish industry looked strong and healthy but that impression hid serious problems. The old traditional industries that were known collectively as 'staple industries' – coal mining, ship building and the production of iron and steel – were boosted by the Great War. After the war these industries went into serious decline and by the mid-1920s Scotland was facing rising unemployment and industrial decline.

Source 4.1

This poster from 1934 captures the mood of people who felt let down by the failed promises and the economic depression of the 1920s. The Labour Party had given hope to many Scots but it, too, had failed to deliver real changes.

The issues developed in the first part of this chapter are summed up here:

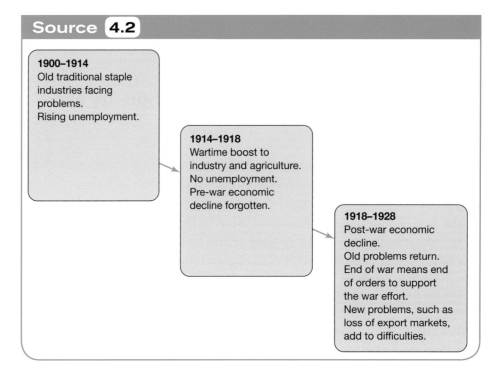

Source 4.2

1900–1914
Old traditional staple industries facing problems.
Rising unemployment.

1914–1918
Wartime boost to industry and agriculture.
No unemployment.
Pre-war economic decline forgotten.

1918–1928
Post-war economic decline.
Old problems return.
End of war means end of orders to support the war effort.
New problems, such as loss of export markets, add to difficulties.

Shipbuilding

Just before war broke out 100,000 workers, or 14 per cent of the adult male working population of Scotland, depended in some way on the shipbuilding industry for their weekly wages. When war did break out the main shipyards on the Clyde – Beardmore, Fairfields and John Brown – were taken under the control of the Royal Navy (the Admiralty) and were therefore under the orders of the Munitions of War Act. For Beardmore, the pre-war naval race came just in time to save it from closure. For a time the earlier difficulties of the shipyards were forgotten but the war brought changes that could not be reversed. The increasing use of new technology and production methods such as automatic machinery and assembly-line production methods increased the speed of production during the war but also threatened jobs. After the war international trade slumped and so did the shipbuilding industry. As orders for new ships dried up, unemployment rose.

Fishing

Looking back, historians of the Scottish fishing industry describe the years around 1900 as 'the glory days'. Huge shoals of herring provided wealth and employment to fishing towns all over the country. By 1913 there were over 10,000 Scottish herring boats and Scotland caught 25 per cent of the UK total.

Small fishing harbours such as Eyemouth, in the Borders, prospered when the railway arrived, opening up markets across Britain. In 1906 Daniel McIver, minister at the EU congregational church in Eyemouth reported,

'The catch landed at Eyemouth this year represents the work of only a hundred boats in all. 1906 is a record year for quantity caught.' (McIver, *An Old Time Fishing Town: Eyemouth*, 1906)

Source 4.3

Part of Eyemouth's herring fleet in the pre-war glory days.

At the peak of the herring boom in 1907, two and a half million barrels of fish were exported – the main markets being Germany, Eastern Europe and Russia. It was reported that Anstruther's harbour became so busy that it was possible to walk from one end of the harbour to the other by stepping from one boat to the next.

In September 1914 Scotland's east coast ports were taken over by the Admiralty. In effect, the North Sea was almost closed to fishing, although restrictions were relaxed as the war went on. During the war the Royal Navy chartered many vessels to use as coastal patrols or for minesweeping. At first these boats were virtually unprotected but by the end of the war sophisticated weapons and detection devices such as radios and hydrophones could be found on many Scottish fishing boats.

The government also wanted to keep the skills of the fishermen and prevent them being swallowed up in the rush to volunteer in the armed forces. The result was the creation of the Royal Navy Volunteer Reserve. The plan was to keep fishermen fishing until the navy had need of their skills to assist in patrolling inshore waters or searching for floating mines (a type of floating bomb).

In 1918 fishermen who had served in the armed forces returned to their old industry hopeful of a bright future. Although the fishing industry did recover the war had created problems. Fuel costs had risen and compensation for boats used in the war effort was seldom enough to repair and equip with new gear. The First World War ended the glory days of the herring fleets. The old export markets in the Baltic, Germany and Russia were gone forever.

Jute

The jute industry is a good example of an industry that was facing some difficulties before the war but which received a huge boost by the war. After the war it faced a rapid decline.

Source 4.4

These Dundee jute workers faced an uncertain future with falling demand after the boom years of the Great War.

Jute fibre was grown mostly in the country we now know as Bangladesh, then part of the British Empire. The jute was exported and Dundee specialised in converting the raw jute fibres into sacking cloth which, in the days before plastics, was used as a container material for almost everything.

The jute industry employed thousands of people in Dundee with 25 per cent of male workers and 67 per cent of female workers dependant on the jute industry for their employment. During the war demand for jute soared as more and more sandbags were needed to line the tops of trenches or provide supports to trench walls. At one point in the war demand topped 6 million sacks in one month. With such demand it is not surprising that profits in the industry rocketed, prompting the *Dundee Advertiser* to report that 'jute fibres have turned into strands of gold', in February 1918. However, the war years could only ever provide a temporary boom. The good times did not last.

Before the war some Dundee businessmen had started to develop the jute industry in the Calcutta area, thereby cutting out Dundee's role in the business. During the war the jute industry in Dundee was protected by a government ban on jute products being processed in Calcutta. When the war ended the jute factories in Dundee were in need of fresh investment and repair. At the same time jute processed in Calcutta was back on the international markets and jute prices fell around the world.

The jute industry illustrated the problem facing British industry at the end of the war.

Run-down machinery and a return to old-fashioned working habits were no match for the new industrial world that emerged from the Great War. Foreign competition forced down prices and took away export markets.

Farming, food and rationing

Source 4.5

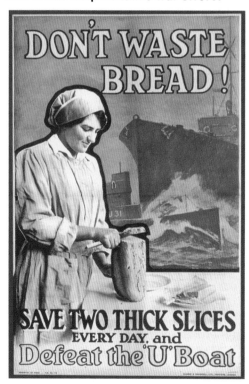

Bread was an essential part of everyone's daily diet. How would eating less bread help Britain's war effort?

In 1914 Britain relied on imports for most of its food. Wheat from the USA and Canada, meat from Australia and South America and butter from New Zealand were just some of the products Britain relied on from overseas. The outbreak of war exposed the difficulties and dangers of that reliance. Germany knew how dependant Britain was on food imports and it launched a submarine campaign against Britain, hoping to starve Britain out of the war. As a result, Britain had to do more to increase food production at home.

Wartime problems

British farming faced problems created by the war, though some problems were more serious than others. It was claimed that the war caused a huge fall in the number of farm workers but this was only partly true. While many men did join the armed forces or seek higher wages in the munitions factories, the actual numbers employed in farming did not fall dramatically.

Source 4.6

Horses were taken from the fields, cities, factories and coal pits of Britain and shipped off to a terrible world.

Admittedly, the total workforce had changed, with many more women, boys and older men taking the place of the usual farm workers. In fact, 30,000 prisoners, 16,000 members of the Women's Land Army and even conscientious objectors worked in agriculture during the war.

A more serious handicap to farming was the army's need for horses, donkeys and mules. During the war almost half a million animals were commandeered from across the country to pull, push and carry on behalf of the war effort. Farms were weakened further by a shortage of fertilisers because the army had priority access to phosphates and nitrogen for the munitions factories.

A good time for farmers?

For many farmers and farm workers the war years were good, with profits and wages rising. In many places farm wages rose by 150 per cent during the war years and at the same time the wages of skilled ploughmen and shepherds doubled. The novel *Sunset Song* describes how a local farmer had 'gone in for the Irish cattle, quick you bought them and quick you sold and reaped a fine profit with prices so brave. He'd made much silver for all that, while the war went on.' (Gibbon, *Sunset Song*, 1996, page 242)

The government tried to increase food production by encouraging the creation of more arable (crop-growing) land. Given Scotland's weather and quality of soil it was less easy for Scottish farmers to convert pasture land into crop-growing ground but Scottish hill farmers did benefit from demand for wool. By 1918 sheep prices were 60 per cent higher than in 1914 and in 1917 the government bought all wool sheared from sheep in the country – the entire 'clip' – to meet the demand for blankets and uniforms for the forces.

Rationing

In spring 1917 food supplies into Britain became a more serious problem when German submarines began targeting all merchant ships carrying food to Britain. For a time the government hoped that asking people for voluntary rationing would help ease the problem. In his *War Memoirs* Lloyd George implied that such voluntary restrictions were successful. He wrote:

 Although there was a degree of scarcity, we were never faced with famine or actual privation. Without general goodwill it would have been impossible to make the regulations effective.

Quoted on www.spartacus.schoolnet.co.uk/FWWrationing.htm

What Lloyd George failed to make clear is that voluntary restrictions failed. Government poster campaigns to 'eat less bread' fell on deaf ears and blind eyes. For those who had money to buy expensive food the cost was a nuisance but not a deterrent. It was the working classes, unable either to find enough food or afford the high prices, who suffered.

By the end of 1917 people began to fear that the country was running out of food.

Source 4.7

Lloyd George 'blew his own trumpet' and claimed his voluntary rationing scheme was a success. Was it?

PUNCH, OR THE LONDON CHARIVARI.—September 5, 1917.

COBBLES LIMITED   FLINT & STEEL

NO COAL   NO MATCHES

COAL MERCHANT   TOBACCONISTS

"KEEP THE HOME FIRES BURNING."
SOLO BY OUR OPTIMISTIC PREMIER.

Charles Young, a soldier on leave in 1917, remembered:

> 66 *You see, us being an island hardly any food could get through, because German U-boats were sinking our food convoys. My family lived on bones from the butcher made into soups. And when some food did get delivered to the shops everyone for miles around besieged the place. The queues stretched for miles, and if you were old or infirm you stood no chance.*
>
> Quoted on www.spartacus.schoolnet.co.uk/FWWrationing.htm

Panic buying led to shortages and so in January 1918 the Ministry of Food decided to introduce rationing. Lloyd George explained the reasons:

> 66 *This rationing system ensured a regular and sufficient food supply and it made it possible for those in charge to calculate with some precision how best they could make the stocks of available food-stuffs go round fairly.*
>
> Quoted on www.spartacus.schoolnet.co.uk/FWWrationing.htm

Although strictly speaking rationing was introduced at different stages for different foodstuffs, full-scale rationing was in force in Scotland by April 1918. The aim was to conserve food supplies, ensure fair distribution and control the rising prices that were becoming a serious concern. As prices rose so did the risk of discontent and demonstrations that would have hindered the war effort. Sugar was the first item to be rationed and this was followed by butcher meat. By the end of the war almost all foods were subject to price control by the government. In some cases rationing even lasted until after the war: for example, sugar and butter remained on ration until 1920.

The land issue in the Highlands and Islands

At the end of the First World War many soldiers and sailors returned to the Highlands and Islands believing that they had been promised land as a reward for fighting for their country. On 28 November 1919 the *Stornoway Gazette* reported a returning soldier saying, 'When we were in the trenches down to our knees in mud and blood we were promised all good things when we should return home victorious.' (Quoted in Royle, *The Flowers of the Forest: Scotland and the Great War*, 2006, page 316)

In 1886 the Crofters Act had guaranteed security of tenure to crofters that meant they could not be evicted from the land they worked on. However, 'the land question' was not solved and difficulties remained. Good quality land was scarce and there were few job opportunities, especially with the collapse of the herring fishing industry. In simple terms crofters and cottars saw ownership of land as a guarantee of security and stability for the future. When land was not immediately available for the ex-servicemen, discontent over the issue grew in the Highlands and Islands once again.

Why did the land issue grow after 1918?

During the war investment and maintenance of large estates had declined. One of the easiest ways for landowners to save money was to allow their arable land to become rough grazing for sheep and cattle, thereby reducing the amount of quality food-growing land available. Returning soldiers who were hoping and, indeed, expecting to be given land as a reward for their sacrifices during the war, were disappointed that this did not happen quickly enough. Many took the law into their own hands and began land raids.

What were land raids?

Land raids usually involved a number of men who marched onto land they believed they should have a right to work on. The men would mark out their farms and hope to gain some publicity and public sympathy for their plight. In the Hebrides, men began to cultivate land and at Drumnadrochit in the Highlands they grazed and reared sheep – in both cases on land that was not their property. Seven men and their families moved from the island of Rona to the island of Raasay and began to cultivate the land. These land raids were illegal yet they created a big problem for the government, as you will find out.

Was land promised for military service?

There is still debate about how justified were the land raiders in expecting land as a reward for serving in the armed forces and much of the debate centres on the exact promises made. It is clear that some of the expectations were based on vague statements made for propaganda or recruitment purposes.

The first point to make is that the returning men believed they had been promised land. Crofter's applying for land on Mull wrote, 'we should like to point out to the Board of Agriculture that the government during the war

made definite promises about settling ex-members of the armed forces on the land.' (Quoted in Macdonald and McFarland, *Scotland and the Great War*, 1998, pages 93–4). Earlier, in 1917, the Duke of Sutherland had added to expectations of land when he made a gift of a large estate farm at Borgie to be used for returning soldiers and sailors who had volunteered for the forces when war broke out.

The Land Settlement Act

The land issue became a major headache for the government but it was, to an extent, of their own creation. In its election manifesto, Lloyd George's Government had stated that it was the duty of the government to provide land for men who had served in the war. With the introduction of the Land Settlement Act in December 1919 it seemed that the government would keep its promise but almost immediately it became clear that they did not have the money needed to do so.

It was one thing to promise land to men who had served in the war but the cost of compulsory purchase of land from the previous owners soon exhausted government reserves. Within five months of the introduction of the Land Settlement Act funds were used up and future plans were suspended. Nevertheless, between 1918 and 1924 the government was under intense pressure to secure land for returning servicemen, even for those who had broken the law by land-raiding.

The land raids continued and the government was still in a difficult position. To meet fully the demand for land resettlement would involve huge expenditure for the government but to do nothing about illegal land raids would also undermine the authority of the government. Their handling of the land raids on Raasay only made a difficult situation worse. The Secretary for Scotland had announced that any land raider would be banned from any official settlement of land but the raiders on Raasay were given temporary accommodation, the Board of Agriculture purchased the raided estate and the raiders were given the land. It now looked as if the government had accepted they could do little to stop the land raiders and would even intervene to solve the problem by giving in to the raiders' demands.

The situation was serious. In 1920 the Board of Agriculture predicted that seizures of land would increase and it reminded the government of its election promise and warned of continuing problems if the promise was not kept. The reply from the government was predictable – they claimed to have not enough money to buy the land needed for resettlement and so the problems lingered on.

Although land raiding had mostly died out by the mid-1920s this did not mean the economic problems of the Highlands had been solved. In 1929 the Committee on Land Settlement in Scotland reported, 'the crofter's conditions were a reproach [disgrace] and the only way to remove that disgrace was to give them the only available land' (Quoted in Devine, *The Scottish Nation: 1700–2007*, 2006, page 446). It was clear that the issue of land settlement had still to be resolved.

Lewis and Leverhulme

The 'Leverhulme Project' and the development of Lewis seemed to promise a lot but also illustrated the difficulty of forcing change on a reluctant society.

In 1919 the island of Lewis was bought by Lord Leverhulme, a man who had made his fortune in the soap business. Later, he added North and South Harris to his possession. Leverhulme hoped to develop both Lewis and Harris and proposed to turn Stornoway into a smart island capital with an expensive war memorial, a cinema and even a railway.

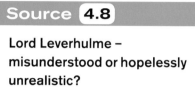

Source 4.8

Lord Leverhulme – misunderstood or hopelessly unrealistic?

In reality, Leverhulme had bought an island facing large-scale emigration, a declining fishing industry and a population struck by tuberculosis, a lung disease unknown in the mid-nineteenth century which was brought over from the mainland cities and which had devastated the island population by 1920.

At the end of the war Lewis was an island in shock. Seven thousand Lewis men served in the armed forces and 17 per cent of them were killed, one of the highest proportions in the UK. The death toll rose further after the war had ended when the 'Iolaire', carrying 284 naval personnel and crew, hit rocks 20 yards from the shore outside Stornoway harbour and 205 were drowned – 175 of them islanders.

When Leverhulme arrived his vision for revival included a new fishing fleet, a more efficient farming base with small holdings reduced in number and a new canning factory in Stornoway. Leverhulme was criticised for being hopelessly out of touch with the situation on Lewis and failing to understand the serious decline in fishing or the islanders' attachment to land.

Scotland at Work and at War

Source 4.9

Lewis suffered heavily even after the end of the war. Did Leverhulme represent insensitive change to a community wanting to re-establish its own way of life?

The clash of interests was illustrated by a land raid on the farms of Coll and Gress. Leverhulme said he needed those two farms to produce milk for the island but raiders declared, 'to fulfill the promise granted by the government to demobilised soldiers and sailors, the land ought to be in wait for us' or, as one islander returning from the war put it, 'Is he willing to give us the land and is he willing to give it now?' (Quoted in Royle, *The Flowers of the Forest: Scotland and the Great War*, 2006, page 317)

The government was in a difficult position. The developments on Lewis were to be funded by Leverhulme's own money. This was a huge bonus for the government but the plans did not satisfy the government's commitment to land settlement. A compromise was reached when land settlement was delayed for 10 years to give Leverhulme:

> *an opportunity of showing whether by the development of his schemes he would convince the Lewis men that it was in their best interests to fall in with his proposals and cease their demands for smallholdings.*
>
> *Quoted in Trevor Royle,* The Flowers of the Forest: Scotland and the Great War, *2006, page 317*

However, the men did not accept Leverhulme's proposals and the land raids continued. Leverhulme retaliated by sacking workers and promising to employ them again only if the raids stopped. Other attempts at compromise failed. Leverhulme even tried to give land to crofters for free but that was rejected by some, fearing they would have to pay higher rates (local taxes) for the land they farmed. Some historians argue that Leverhulme was finally disillusioned not by the islanders' refusal to work in his factory but by their rejection of the offer of free land. Leverhulme suspended all of his projects in Lewis in September 1923 and turned his attention to Harris but by then he was ill and he died in 1925.

Debate continues over the Leverhulme project. Investment of private money was desperately needed after the war but the supporters of the land raids believed that Leverhulme did not understand the Highland way of life and attachment to the land, arguing that he would have reduced the island way of life to factory work. Ironically, high unemployment when the project collapsed led thousands of islanders to emigrate, with many finding employment in the car factories of Detroit and Chicago.

After the failure of Leverhulme's project other investors avoided the Highlands and the situation was not helped by the anti-Highland reporting in many of the lowland newspapers which encouraged the stereotype of the lazy, work-shy Gael who refused to enter the modern industrial world.

Migration

For many Scots the only answer to Scotland's postwar problems was the old escape route of emigration. In the 1920s emigration from Scotland became a flood and between 1921 and 1931 Scotland's total population fell for the first time after a century of steady increase. In the inter-war period Scotland had the highest rate of emigration of any European country. It was said at the time that Scotland was being emptied of its population, its spirit, its wealth, its industry and its talent. In the Highlands the population fell by 16,000, despite subsidies from the government to ease the land problem. However, it would be wrong to think that only the Highlands were affected by emigration. Lowland Scotland also saw a huge outpouring of skilled labour.

Of course, emigration was not new. By the late-nineteenth century emigration across the Atlantic to the USA and Canada had increased, partly as a result of shorter travelling times. This was an important concern to workers who could not afford to lose earnings on a long voyage. Another reason for high emigration was the active promotion of Canada as a destination for Scottish migrants. By the 1890s the Canadian government had two full-time agents working in Scotland, touring agricultural fairs, exhibitions and any place where large numbers of people were gathered. One of the agents could even give presentations in Gaelic. By the 1920s full-time resident agents encouraging emigration to Canada had offices in Glasgow and Inverness.

Emigration was boosted by the Empire Settlement Act of 1922 which was intended to boost the rural populations of Canada and other parts of the British Empire. Subsidies were paid to emigrants who agreed to work the land for a certain amount of time. Both town and country workers seized the opportunity to escape from the grip of depression and unemployment in Scotland. In April 1923, 600 Hebrideans embarked on two Canadian Pacific liners at Lochboisdale and Stornoway, with most of them taking

Scotland at Work and at War

advantage of the Empire Settlement Act to secure subsidised passages to Canada. The move offered them the chance to become independent landowners rather than continue to struggle amidst the declining farming opportunities in Scotland.

Many urban industrial workers found it difficult to adapt to the harsh realities of farming but not all of them intended to stay in Canada! It did not take long for emigrants from urban Scotland to realise that a subsidised voyage to Canada could be a practical, if often illegal, route into the back door of the industrialised north-east of the USA.

The Salvation Army also played a part in migration from Scotland and, in fact, claimed to be the world's largest emigration agency. It provided assisted passages and employment advice for single women, unemployed men and young people. Between 1872 and 1930 Quarrier's Orphan Homes of Scotland helped to arrange the migration of 7000 children to Ontario as part of its wider programme of rescue and rehabilitation. For many of the orphan children emigration provided the fresh start they needed but controversy remains around how much choice they really had in their migration.

Some historians argue that the figures for migration should be balanced with the figures of those returning. Although about one-third of emigrants did return to Scotland, the 1920s saw an 'out migration' from Scotland higher than at any other time in Scotland's history. Whether or not these migrants returned does not matter as much as the fact that they all saw migration as an escape from a country locked in unemployment and decline.

Source 4.10

By the end of the 1930s 250,000 people had been settled overseas by the Salvation Army.

It is hard to believe from this photo but one-third of all emigrants returned home.

WE'VE GOT JOBS IN CANADA
WE DON'T WANT THE DOLE!

Conclusion

In Scotland, the years after the war are associated with economic depression and high unemployment. To an extent Scotland was paying for the artificial boom of the war years. The old staple industries of Scotland were facing difficulties long before 1914 but people have short memories and the decline of the early 1920s hit hard. Edwin Muir wrote in his *Scottish Journey* in the early 1930s:

> *Now Scotland's industry, like its intelligence before it, is gravitating towards England but its population is sitting where it did before in the company of disused coal pits and silent ship yards.*
>
> *By 1933 the Clyde was launching merely 56,000 tons of shipping, and the coal industry was finding work for only 80,000 hands and producing a third less coal than in 1913.*
>
> *The Dundee jute trade was deeply depressed and the Borders woollen industry for the greater part of the year was on part-time working.*
>
> *The output of Scottish farming was falling while it was still rising in England, and in the fishing industry the numbers of those employed and the value of the catch were both steadily dropping.*

Edwin Muir, Scottish Journey, 1996 (first published 1935)

Scotland faced hard times.

Activities

Work in pairs. You should each make up at least 10 questions which you would use to test someone's understanding of the issues, the people and the events surrounding the Highlands, the land issue and migration after the war.

To construct your questions you must first understand the issues you are assessing and ensure your questions are not vague, ambiguous and that they focus attention on the main points. One-word-answer questions such as 'who was…' or 'when was…' are not allowed!

Your questions should be mature, well presented and test real understanding. The purpose is to help learning, not to catch people out with really obscure or tricky questions.

When you have both completed 10 questions, try them out on each other. Can your partner answer your questions? And can you answer your partner's questions in return? When you have finished you should focus on the questions you could not answer – these are the areas you will need to work on a little more when you are revising.

Repeat this exercise either now or at a later date – and try using different topics.

5 Political Change during the War

What effect did the war have on Scottish politics?

In 1914 the UK had a Liberal government and in Scotland the Liberals were the most powerful political party. The Conservative and Unionist Party was much less important and represented mainly rural areas and especially the wealthy land-owning class. The Labour Party had not yet made any significant breakthrough into national politics.

By 1918 the landscape of British and Scottish politics had changed completely. The Liberal Party had split and after the mid-1920s they would never again be a significant force in British politics. The Conservative and Unionist Party recovered from its poor pre-war election results and began to attract new voters from the middle classes in the cities. The Independent Labour Party was stronger in 1918 than it had been in 1914 and the mainstream Labour Party was about to become one of the two big parties in British politics.

The decline of the Liberals

Put simply, the war split the Liberal Party. Even at the start of the war the Liberal Party was divided over the issue of going to war. The Liberal Party had traditionally opposed British involvement in wars and the issue caused some Liberal politicians to resign. They went on to form the Union of Democratic Control which became one of the main anti-war organisations in Britain.

MPs who had opposed the war found it very difficult to get the co-operation of local party members. One MP, Arthur Ponsonby, had spoken out against the war so much that the party was unwilling to allow him to stand as the Liberal candidate at the next election.

Arguments within the party weakened its organisation and demoralised party workers. Party funds collapsed as members stopped paying subscriptions. In November 1918, with the election approaching, Aberdeen Liberals stated that 'unless additional subscriptions were obtained it would be impossible to appoint organisers.' (Quoted in Macdonald and McFarland, *Scotland and the Great War*, 1998, page 43)

As the war progressed the ideas that were at the heart of Liberalism were abandoned. Initially, Prime Minister Asquith had a 'business as usual'

attitude to the war and most people believed the conflict would be over by Christmas. However, as the war dragged on it became more and more obvious that direct government intervention in the economy, in industry and even in people's everyday lives would become necessary. The old non-interventionist ideals of Liberalism were fading fast and the 'in fighting' of Liberal politicians was weakening the party. To make matters worse, the introduction of conscription led to bitter arguments in the Liberal party. Such government intervention was against the basic ideas of Liberalism.

The party was weakened also by the shell scandal. By early 1915 British Army Commander Sir John French had complained that British attacks were failing because of a lack of ammunition, particularly artillery shells. His comments were reported by both the *Times* and *The Daily Mail* in articles about the 'shell scandal'. It was suggested that the scandal was encouraged in the press by Lloyd George, an ambitious rival to Asquith but who was not yet ready to challenge for power. He said 'The Prime Minister has been so good to me that I would never be disloyal to him in the smallest detail.' (Quoted on www.spartacus.schoolnet.co.uk/PRasquith.htm) Whether there really was a shell scandal or not did not matter. The reports in the press that reached the public suggested the Liberals were a party that could not run the war effort on their own and who needed the Conservatives to help them.

Source 5.1

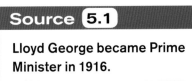

Lloyd George became Prime Minister in 1916.

A new coalition government was formed in May 1915 in which Lloyd George was minister for munitions but by December 1916 the ill feeling between Asquith and Lloyd George had reached a peak. The situation became so bad that the King asked Lloyd George to form a new coalition government and, in December 1916, Lloyd George replaced Asquith as prime minister. When the war ended, Lloyd George wanted to make his own position stronger and he took advantage of the atmosphere of relief at the end of the war in order to call an election.

The Coupon Election

The 'Coupon Election' took place on 14 December 1918. In an attempt to make clear for voters exactly what any Liberal candidate stood for, all supporters of the coalition were given a letter of support from Lloyd George and Andrew Bonar Law, leader of the Conservatives. Asquith described the letter as a 'coupon' and the name stuck.

All 159 Liberal candidates supporting Lloyd George were given the 'coupon' and an arrangement was made that where a 'coupon' Liberal stood for election, no Conservative would challenge him. Where a Conservative stood, no 'coupon' Liberal challenged him. Therefore there was no chance of coalition candidates competing against another. All 159 'Lloyd George' Liberals won and most Liberals without 'the coupon' lost. Even Asquith lost his seat for East Fife.

By 1924 the Liberals were reduced to only eight MPs in Scotland, five of them from the Highlands and Islands. Even the morning newspapers in Scotland's cities had become Tory (conservative) supporters. The Liberal party could no longer rely on Scotland's old traditional radical, reformist traditions for support. Tom Devine illustrates the decline in the attraction of the Liberals and the values they represented:

 A significant press development was the transformation of the widely read People's Journal from a powerful radical [supporting social reform] weekly full of social comment to an outlet for sentimental stories and knitting patterns.

Tom Devine, The Scottish Nation *1700–2007, 2006, page 315*

Scottish politics had become split between the left and the right and perhaps a more cynical view of politicians grew. In *Sunset Song*, written in the 1930s, the Liberal candidate in Kinraddie was described as:

 An oldish creature from Glasgow, fell rich he was, folk said, with as many ships to his name as others had fields. And real Radical he was, with everybody's money but his own.

Lewis Grassic Gibbon, Sunset Song, *1996, page 96 (first published 1932)*

For many Scots the Liberals had simply ceased to matter.

The rise of the Labour Party

In the 1914 election Labour gained almost 800,000 votes but by 1918 support for Labour had increased to well over 2,000,000 votes and the party gained one-third of all votes cast in Scotland. By the mid-1920s the Labour Party had replaced the Liberals as one of the two big political parties.

One main reason for Labour's increasing influence is that the electorate – and potential Labour voters – had increased. In 1918 the right to vote was

given to all men over the age of 21 and women over 30. For the first time, almost the entire male population were given the vote on the basis of age, rather than the property they owned or rented. Consequently, a huge number of working-class men – and women over 30 – gained the vote for the first time. The extension of the franchise to include women could also explain the growth of the Labour Party. Some historians argue that women had become politicised on the Clyde as a result of the rent strikes and many women, among them Mary Barbour, Agnes Dollan and Helen Crawfurd, proved to be very effective local councillors.

Labour benefited from the change in the voting behaviour of the Irish Catholic voters who had deserted the Liberals after 1916. In that year a rising of Irish rebels in Dublin had at first attracted little national support in Ireland but the brutal and repressive policies of the Government afterwards had infuriated Catholics in Ireland and Scotland.

The *Catholic Observer* wrote:

 The formation of a powerful Labour Party gives us an opportunity. The Labour Party is indeed and in truth the people's party. And as a vast majority of Irish in Great Britain are toilers [ordinary working people] it is to that party they turn.

Tom Devine, The Scottish Nation 1700–2007, 2006, page 312–13

Source 5.2

The Labour Party benefited from the radicalisation of Scottish politics during the war. This photo looks like a mothers' outing but the banner shows it to be a left-wing group of Communist supporters from Methil. Many of these women would vote for the first time in 1918 – and many voted Labour.

Another reason for Labour's growth lies with the work of the Independent Labour Party (ILP) in Scotland.

The Independent Labour Party (ILP)

After 1884 and the Third Reform Act thousands of working-class men had the right to vote but there was no party to represent directly working-class interests. MPs were not paid for their work so even if a working-class man could be elected he would not be able to support himself and his family. The answer seemed to lie with the Liberals who supported, and even sponsored, many Lib/Lab candidates, as the combined Liberal and Labour candidates came to be called. Not everyone was happy with this arrangement and increasingly there were calls for a separate party to be created that would represent the interests of the labouring classes.

The Independent Labour Party was formed in 1893 as a political party genuinely independent of the Liberals. By 1900, assorted left-wing groups, among them the ILP, helped to create the Labour Representation Committee which soon became known as the Labour Party. Nevertheless, the ILP remained a separate and influential political party, especially in Scotland.

Source 5.3

This ILP poster emphasises the international socialist idea that workers of the world should unite to campaign for their common interests.

In Chapter 3 you read that the ILP took a strong anti-war position and led campaigns against conscription. The ILP was active in the anti-conscription movement and the party leadership in Scotland opposed Britain's involvement in the First World War. On the industrial front, ILP members were actively involved in resisting the Munitions Act of 1915 and in opposing the introduction of dilution. However, these factors do not explain fully the ILP's popularity. Out of 19 ILP local councillors elected during the war years, only two of them were publicly against the war. While the ideology of the ILP was socialist, their campaigns were aimed at local issues. John Wheatley, later an ILP MP, wrote, 'at our meetings we talked local politics advocating the claims of the East End of Glasgow rather than the Near East of Europe' meaning they worked to improve local conditions for working class people rather than discuss international issues that were of little immediate concern. (Quoted in Devine, *The Scottish Nation 1700–2007*, 2006, page 313)

Both the ILP and the Labour party campaigned for housing reform after the war. This was an effective campaign target as even a Unionist survey of public opinion revealed housing as the number one public concern. Prime Minister Lloyd George had promised 'homes fit for heroes to live in' but little seemed to be changing.

Red Clydeside

Between 1915 and 1919 parts of Glasgow and its surrounding area became known as 'Red Clydeside'. To most of those people involved in the protests, the unrest on the Clyde was the result of unfair rent rises and the worry of skilled working men seeing their jobs and their futures under threat. To the government and a worried middle class, the protests that grew up from 1915 onwards in the shipyards, tenement kitchens and munitions factories of the Glasgow area were signs that a communist revolution was on its way.

Source 5.4

Did the red flag flying really mean the Clyde had gone 'Red'?

In reality there were two phases to 'Red Clydeside'. The first phase was triggered in 1915 by the confrontation between engineers and the Ministry of Munitions over the issue of dilution and also by the rent strikes. The second phase took place just after the war ended. Strikes and conflict between workers and police in George Square, Glasgow, caused Robert Munro, the Scottish Secretary, to warn the government that a Communist revolution was brewing in Glasgow.

Even before the war started new working practices and mass production methods were changing the huge engineering factories around Glasgow. Older machines needed skilled men to operate them. New machines needed only a 'machine-minder' – a low-paid boy or woman. Processes were being re-organised and speeded up on mass-production lines. Men who had served long apprenticeships and prided themselves on their craftsmanship now worried about their futures. These worries were made worse when war broke out and the government demanded more and more output, especially of munitions. To meet the demand even more new technology and working methods were introduced. Jobs that had once been skilled were broken down into separate processes, each process being done by a less well-trained and less well-paid worker – even a woman!

The tension over the use of unskilled women workers was expressed in a resolution passed by the Amalgamated Society of Engineers (ASE) which declared that 'no woman shall be put to work a lathe [a specialist machine], and if this were done the men would know how to protect their rights.'

The workers and their trades unions called this issue dilution. What dilution meant was the use of unskilled workers to do parts of a job that had previously been done only by skilled men. In other words the skills (and wages that went with that skill) were being lessened or diluted by the use of unskilled labour.

The fears of workers in the engineering works were increased by the appointment of William Weir as controller of munitions for Scotland. Weir had a reputation for being a hard man who disliked trades unions. Early in 1915 the workers at Fairfield Shipbuilding and Engineering Company went on strike for an extra two pennies an hour. The Fairfield workers were also concerned about Weir's employment of American engineers in local factories who were paid higher wages than the Scottish workers. Although the strike was soon settled, the scene had been set for future trouble. Tension increased with the introduction of leaving certificates which meant that workers now had to get permission to leave one job before they could get another and the engineers felt this was another attempt to control not only what jobs they did, but also where they worked. By 1915 tension and suspicion between workers and government was high.

The rent strikes of 1915 are dealt with elsewhere in this book but the strikes were part of the unsettling effect of the war on the Glasgow area. From the workers' point of view the rent strikes had been hugely successful – the government had backed down and a Rent Restriction Act had met the demands of the strikers. The women had also been supported by strikes in engineering factories and munitions works. One reason the government had restricted rents was to avoid any further disruption to munitions production. A lesson had been learned from the rent strikes – united action that threatened the flow of munitions would make the government sit up and take notice of strikers' demands.

Source 5.5

The masthead of the Clyde Workers' Committee newspaper.

The government took a different view. They could accept the fairness of the women's demands in the rent strike and the settlement reached was fair. However, the government was very sensitive to any threat to wartime production. By 1915 the demand for more and more munitions soared. The government became very suspicious of any attempt by workers to form themselves into groups that might pose a threat to smooth wartime production. Such a group was the Clyde Workers' Committee (CWC). Trade union leaders Willie Gallacher and David Kirkwood, along with socialist John Maclean, soon became the centre of government suspicion. These men were able to attract crowds of thousands to political rallies. The government worried that these people could undermine the war effort and lead Glasgow towards revolution.

Strikes had already been banned by the Defence of the Realm Act and the Munitions of War Act but the CWC organised small-scale strikes to protest at the removal of workers' rights. The government wanted to cool things down so David Lloyd George, government minister in charge of munitions production, came north to meet CWC leaders and engineering workers on Christmas Day 1915. The mainstream popular newspapers reported the meeting as 'good humoured' but the ILP's newspaper, *Forward*, reported more accurately that 'the vast overwhelming majority of the meeting was angry'. (*Forward*, 1 January 1916) The government reacted by closing down *Forward* for a time. From the government's point of view the CWC was a nest of revolutionaries ready to upset the war effort and even lead revolution in Britain.

Early in 1916 the government acted to enforce dilution. When strikes broke out leaders such as Kirkwood were arrested, imprisoned and even taken away from the Clyde. Some, like John Maclean, were imprisoned in Edinburgh Castle or banned from returning to Glasgow.

Unrest continued. For some time the ILP and other groups had campaigned against conscription and when it was introduced in the summer of 1916 many workers saw yet another threat to jobs. They felt workers would be conscripted and, under the rules of 'work of national importance', be sent back to the factories to work but this time under direct government control. When more strikes broke out the government took strong action and public opinion supported the government. Newspapers

Source 5.6

Kirkwood and Gallacher are arrested for defending worker's rights – or undermining the war effort?

described the strikers as being greedy, ignorant and selfish when 'their thoughts and energy should be absorbed in the work of the great war'. A letter written by a member of the public summed up how many people felt:

 Four thousand callous [hard hearted] men put the lives of our brave men in jeopardy [danger] by stopping work. Now is the time to get rid of them. The place for them is the army!

Quoted in Trevor Royle, The Flowers of the Forest: Scotland and the Great War, 2006, page 239

Through 1917 and 1918 the area was relatively calm but Red Clydeside was about to become unsettled again as the war ended.

For some time there had been growing support for a campaign to reduce the working week of 54 hours, partly to help create jobs for soldiers returning from fighting. Prime Minister Lloyd George had promised troops returning from the First World War 'a land fit for heroes.' Instead, most soldiers were disillusioned. Some people believe that the Russian revolution of late 1917 had inspired some workers to believe that great change was possible. Faced with bad housing and unemployment, workers and soldiers alike wanted change.

The Clyde Workers Committee initially suggested a 30-hour working week based upon a six-hour working day, a five-day week and a wage of one pound per day. Eventually a compromise demand for a 40-hour working week was agreed but the CWC promised that if a 40-week did not absorb the unemployed, 'a more drastic reduction of hours will be demanded'. Either way the employers were not too happy about paying wages when fewer hours were worked.

Source 5.7

The beginning of the strike – or the start of a revolution?

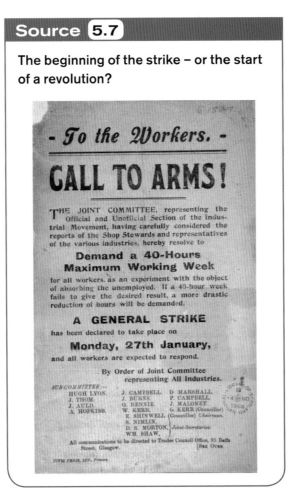

By Monday 27 January 1919 there was huge support for a call for strike action in the area. All of the big factories came out on strike and support grew outside Glasgow. For example, 1500 Lanarkshire miners took strike action and Belfast was brought to a standstill.

On the Friday of that week workers began to assemble in George Square, Glasgow. As the crowd grew, police were lined up in streets around the Square. It is estimated that at least 90,000 people were in the Square when the police launched a baton charge on the crowd. One view is that the police attack was completely unprovoked. Another view argues the strikers were forcibly stopping trams running along beside the Square. Others argue that the crowd was seen as a revolutionary mob and when there were reports of a red flag flying over the crowd the government had to take action. It was only 14 months since the Russian Revolution and, in the same month as the meeting in George Square, the German Revolution was in progress.

A running battle started between the police and demonstrators. Iron railings and bottles were used as a defence against the police truncheons. The fighting spread towards Glasgow Green where the police were waiting but the strikers chased them off. Fighting continued for the rest of the day and into the night, though it is believed that the government exaggerated the seriousness of the events.

Over 12,000 English troops were brought in by the government to restore order. Scottish soldiers stationed at Maryhill Barracks in Glasgow were not used for fear they might not obey orders to turn their guns on the strikers if necessary. Six tanks were also available for use and machine gun posts were set up in the city.

Within a week of the battle at George Square, the strike was over. Although the aim of a 40-hour working week had not been achieved, the striking workers from the engineering and shipbuilding industries returned to work with an agreement that guaranteed them a 47-hour working week – 10 hours less than before the strike. This was a victory for the workers in the short term but did not seriously challenge the role of the bosses.

Source 5.8

Willie Gallagher

Was there ever a risk of revolution on the Clyde?

There is little evidence that the leaders of the strikes and demonstrations ever considered challenging the authority of the British government. Even at Glasgow's May Day rally, with a crowd of almost 100,000 people, the declared aim of the ILP was for 'A Living Wage for all and Justice for our Soldiers and their Dependants.' That was hardly a revolutionary statement.

Later, Willie Gallacher said the demonstrators should have marched to the Maryhill Barracks and tried to persuade the troops stationed there to come out on the protesters' side. Perhaps the huge crowds could have been persuaded to support more revolutionary demands but as Gallagher later

said, they were carrying on a strike when they ought to have been making a revolution. However, for most of the strikers and demonstrators the protests on the Clyde only ever had limited aims. Worries about dilution or high rents motivated the protests, not desire for revolution.

The myth of Red Clydeside grew in later years with the rise in support for the Labour Party and the decline of the Liberals.

The 1922 election and beyond

Source 5.9

The Independent Labour Party made its electoral breakthrough in 1922, when it won ten out of the fifteen Glasgow parliamentary seats and sent a total of 29 Scottish MPs to Westminster.

In 1922 Labour finally achieved the breakthrough they had been hoping for but for many Scots it was a breakthrough for the ILP. Forty out of the total of 43 prospective Labour candidates were members of the ILP. In Glasgow, the party, including several of the Red Clydesiders, won ten out of the fifteen parliamentary constituency seats in the city. Some people might argue that the rise of Labour in Scotland had much to do with Red Clydeside. What is clear is that the Great War had changed the political makeup of Scotland.

At its peak in the mid-1920s ILP membership in Scotland accounted for a third of all membership of the party in Britain and out of a total over just over 1000 branches throughout Britain, over 300 were in Scotland. For many Scots in the 1920s, especially around Clydeside, the ILP was the Labour Party.

For Labour supporters and socialists across Scotland it seemed as if a new political world was opening up. MP James Maxton had declared his intentions to 'make English-ridden, capitalist-ridden Scotland into the Scottish socialist Commonwealth' and David Kirkwood, a socialist, wrote in his autobiography, *My Life of Revolt* (1935):

> *Glasgow was ringing with the message of Socialism. Within a week of the election day, it seemed likely that the whole team of eleven would win and that Socialism would be triumphant. There we were, men who a few years before had been scorned, some of us in jail, now being the men to whom the people pinned their faith.*
>
> Quoted on www.spartacus.schoolnet.co.uk/TUkirkwoodD.htm

For Scottish socialists the early 1920s were days of hope but by the 1930s things had changed. By then the ILP was disillusioned with the Labour Party. They claimed the Labour Party in parliament had sold out on its socialist principles to gain political power. In 1932 the ILP broke its links with the Labour Party forever.

Activities

You are an engineer on Clydeside in 1916.

Design a fly-poster outlining why you are on strike:

- What are your grievances?
- Why do you feel strike action is legitimate given that the country is at war?
- What do you hope to achieve?

Think about what images you want to include in your poster and what essential information must be there.

Activities

You are the Secretary for Scotland in 1919.

You are preparing a statement for release to the press explaining why you think the government should take action against 'Red Clydeside' in early 1919.

- How will you persuade members of the public to support you?
- How will you justify the use of force?
- What techniques will you use to move support away from the strikers and over to your side?

Scotland after the War

The significance of the Great War in the development of Scottish identity

'For King and Country'. That epitaph marks thousands of war memorials and is prominent also on the scroll marking the death of every soldier that was sent to their families. The kilted regiments were proud to wear the tartan but the cause they fought for was British, not Scottish. Although a small group of nationalists campaigned for Scotland to be represented at the Treaty of Versailles in order to assert the right of a small nation to self determination, few Scots cared much about the issue.

Before the war most Scots were happy to be part of the 'Workshop of the World' and benefited from a union with England. Only a few, mostly 'Young Scots', campaigned for Home Rule and in the flush of patriotic togetherness that flooded over Britain in August 1914, the Scottish Home Rule Bill was abandoned by parliament. Power was still in the hands of London-based central government and despite pressure for changes in the way Scotland was governed, most Scots were happy to remain part of Great Britain.

Source 6.1

This parade of sea scouts in the 1920s represents the awareness of separate national identities but also the willingness to operate within a United Kingdom. In the post-war years there was no large desire for Scottish independence.

In 1918 the Labour Party's election manifesto promised to fight for 'The Self-Determination of the Scottish People' and 'The Complete Restoration of the Land of Scotland to the Scottish People' but those proposals did not catch the public's imagination or support. Although Scottish Home Rule was still a politically live issue in the 1920s, it failed to set the heather on fire. The Scottish Council of the Labour Party declared that the Labour Party in Scotland should aim to secure the establishment of a Scottish parliament but the Labour Party's commitment to Home Rule faded after the collapse of the short-lived Labour Government of 1924. In the 1920s all three major parties actively supported the union and Home Rule bills in parliament in 1924 and 1927 went nowhere. Nevertheless, there were some who continued to campaign actively for an independent Scotland and in the 1920s economic distress made more people listen to the arguments for independence.

The inter-war years were times of high unemployment and poverty and there were some Scots who believed that the union within the UK was no longer helpful to Scotland.

Scots no longer saw England and the Empire as being able to provide resources and leadership to overcome the economic and social problems affecting Scotland. Migration to England or the Empire no longer promised a brighter future and Scotland was no longer the workshop of the Empire. During the inter-war period, large-scale unemployment increased in traditional heavy industries such as shipbuilding, textiles and coal mining. Central government was blamed for doing very little.

At the same time there was a division between the old-style Home Rulers who had their roots in the later-Victorian period and the more radical nationalists whose purpose was to resist the erosion of Scottish culture and Scottish identity by the spread of 'Englishness' in all aspects of life. Artists, writers and poets such as Hugh MacDiarmid styled themselves as a 'Scottish Literary Renaissance' and took pride in their attacks on those who, in their view, had sold out to England.

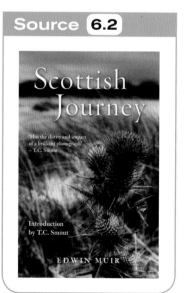

Source 6.2

In May 1928 the National Party of Scotland was founded. Its chairman and secretary, Roland Muirhead and John MacCormick, had grown up politically in the Independent Labour Party but by then the political militancy of the Central Belt had faded. MacCormick and Muirhead received only 3000 votes in the 1929 General Election, less than five per cent of the vote in each

constituency. In 1931 things were no better. The most successful candidate only polled fourteen per cent of the vote.

In 1914 Scotland seemed prosperous and positive, a valued part of the UK at the heart of the British Empire. Twenty years later, Edwin Muir travelled around Scotland and reported:

> *The conclusion that I have come to after seeing what I saw of Scotland was the fundamental cause of its many ills was economic not national. It has happened because Scotland is at the edge of an economic circle, whose centre is London.*
>
> *Edwin Muir,* Scottish Journey, *1996, page 248 (first published 1935)*

But Muir did not see nationalism as the answer alone:

> *The nationalists argue the partnership is a bad one for Scotland but if the nationalists ideas were put into practice there would still be unemployment, the slums would still exist as they are, the great majority of the population would still be poor, the working man would still live in fear of being thrown out of his job.*

Muir saw the problems of Scotland as economic. Emotional nationalism would not help that:

> *The population would have the comfort of knowing they were citizens of an independent Scotland, of being poor on Scottish money instead of English, of drawing the dole [unemployment benefit] from a Scottish government instead of an English one. The upper middle classes are being anglicised not because they prefer England to Scotland but because an English accent and English manners are of more economic and social value in present day society than a Scottish accent and Scottish manners.*

Muir concluded that hanging on to an illusion of the past would not help:

> *An enormous change must happen. Scotland, with its derelict industries, its vast slums, its depopulated glens… and its army of unemployed has no future save through such a change.*

Edwin Muir, Scottish Journey, *1996, pages 246–50 (first published 1935)*

In the years after the Great War Scotland had to come to terms with the reality that had been growing before 1914. Scottish industry was in decline and only temporarily rescued by the boom years of the war. After 1918 many Scots tried to escape, either to England or further away. The old Scotland had been shaken up by the war and would not settle down to the old certainties again.

Sunset Song was published in 1932 and the novel captured a Scotland that was vanishing. The change was acknowledged in the final funeral scene when the minister of Kinraddie spoke of the four local men who had died in the war:

> *And the minister began to speak again, his voice ringing out over the loch.*
> *"They went quiet and brave from the land they loved. With them died a thing older than ourselves, the last of the old scots folk. They died for a world that is past, but they did not die for this that we seem to inherit"*

Lewis Grassic Gibbon, Sunset Song, *1996, page 256 (first published 1932)*

The optimism and excitement of 1914 had long since gone.

Activities

Scotland in 1928

Your challenge is to produce a display showing the main features of Scotland in 1928 as they apply to your course of study – in the same way that you created a display for Scotland in 1914 at the beginning of this book.

Your display or presentation must make people want to stop and look at your views of Scotland in 1928.

Work in a group of no more than four. Your teacher will give you an appropriate time scale for the task.

continued →

Your display or presentation should deal with the following topics:

- changes in industry
- changes in politics
- changes in the Highlands
- the war and the price Scotland paid
- how Scotland remembers the war.

Success criteria

Somewhere in your display or presentation each topic should have:

- a text box with three sentences explaining your ideas
- one illustration – or two if you want to show different points of view
- a smart slogan summarising the core issue associated with the topic.

Your display must be visible across a classroom. It must use at least three colours and must use at least two different sizes of text. Think creatively – who said it has to be paper based?

Conclusions

In your groups, compare your displays from 1914 and 1918 and compile a list of changes.

Each group should agree on five main changes (one for each topic).

Your teacher could collect a change for each topic from each group and display them so that the whole class can see them.

Extended writing task

Using your list of changes, each person should write a short essay of several paragraphs with the title 'How far did the Great War change Scotland?' – think widely!

Preparing for Paper 2 of the Higher History Exam

Paper 2 of your Higher History exam is based entirely on source analysis. The exam paper will be divided into five special topics. This book is about **ONE** of those special topics: Scotland and the Impact of the Great War 1914–1928.

What will Paper 2 of my exam be about?

You have to answer ONE special topic section.

You must answer the questions set on the special topic you have studied.

There will be questions on other special topics that other candidates have studied. Make sure you answer the correct special topic.

Your special topic syllabus is divided into six main sections. Check out the Arrangements document at http://www.sqa.org.uk/sqa/files_ccc/History_Higher_2010.pdf. There you will find the detailed content of the special topic 'Scotland and the Impact of the Great War 1914–1928'.

The first section you will see is called 'Background'. The last section is called 'Perspective'. Neither of those sections will have any questions asked about them. They are **NOT** examined. That leaves four other sections, called issues, and each one of those issues has a question linked to it.

What do I have to do?

You will have five sources to use and four questions to answer. You will have 1 hour and 25 minutes to do that. That means you will have about 20 minutes to deal with each question so answers must be well structured and well developed. Put simply, that means you must do three things in each question:

1. **You must do what you are asked to do.**

2. **You must refer to information in the source.**

3. **You must also include your own relevant recalled knowledge.**

Each question also has its own particular process you must use to answer it successfully.

Later in this section there are sample answers to show you how to deal with the different questions.

What types of questions will I be asked?

There are **FOUR** different types of question. Each type will be in your exam paper.

Important: In this book the questions are listed as Type 1, 2, 3 and 4. This does **NOT** mean the questions will appear in that order in the exam. The different types of question can appear in **ANY** order.

> Question Type 1 is a source evaluation question worth 5 marks.

It will usually be identified with a question asking 'How useful is Source A as evidence …?'

In this type of question you are being asked to **judge** how good the source is as a piece of **historical evidence**:

- You will get up to a maximum of **2 marks** for writing about the source's origin (who wrote it or where the source first appeared) and its purpose (why the source was produced).

- You will only get up to **1 mark** by identifying and commenting briefly on where the source is from and why it was produced.

- For **2 marks** you will be expected to explain why its origin and purpose is important in the context of the question.

You will get up to a maximum of **2 marks** for **explaining why** the parts of the source you have selected are **useful** in terms of the question:

- There are no marks for just copying chunks of the source.

- Just listing relevant points from the source will only gain **1 mark**.

- For **2 marks** you must mention a point from the source and ALSO explain why the evidence you have selected is relevant to the question.

- Watch out for how that works in the examples that follow.

You will get up to a maximum of **2 marks** for using your own **detailed knowledge** as long as it is relevant to the question. This is called using relevant recall:

- You might, for example, want to consider if the source is entirely useful. A source will seldom be entirely valuable or useful. It will have limitations and it's up to you to explain what these limits to usefulness are.

- In this case a useful word to use is **'partly'**!

- You can give evidence to show that the source has its uses but also include information to suggest the source does not give the whole picture.

This looks like the total number of marks available for the question comes to 6, but there is only a possible total of 5 marks for this question. Stop to think how this helps you. If you had a weak section on origin and purpose you might only get 1 mark out of 2. But if your other two sections are well done, gaining the maximum of 2 marks per part, then you can still achieve the maximum total of 5 marks.

> Question Type 2 is a Comparison Question worth 5 Marks.

You will be asked to compare two points of view overall and in detail. It might **NOT** use the word 'compare' in the question.

The wording of the question might be something like 'To what extent does Source B agree with Source C about…?'

You will get up to a maximum of **2 marks** for an **overall comparison**. That means you should outline the main ideas or opinions or points of view in the two sources.

You will get up to a maximum of **4 marks** by **developing** your comparison in **detail**.

To get all 4 marks it is *not enough* just to list points of difference between the sources. In fact you might get **NO MARKS** for simply stating 'Source B says… but Source C says …'

- You **MUST** show that you understand the points made in the sources and explain in what ways they differ from each other or support each other.

- When you are explaining the differences or similarities it would be a good idea to use your own detailed knowledge to support your answer.

- There will always be **4** points of comparison for you to find in the sources.

- You will get **NO MARKS** for 'ghost' comparisons. In other words, no marks for writing 'Source B says… but Source C makes no mention of this.'

Question Type 3 is a 'How far…' Question and is worth 10 Marks.

This question is to test your knowledge on one specific part of an issue, called a sub-issue. You can find all the sub-issues in the column called 'detailed descriptors' on the SQA syllabus website. The web address is given earlier in this chapter.

For example, a question that asks 'How far does Source B explain the reasons why so many Scotsmen joined the army in 1914?' tests your knowledge of the reasons for voluntary recruitment.

To answer this question you must show you have **understood the reasons** for joining up that are included in the source and be able to explain those reasons. You can get up to **4 marks** just by doing that.

You must **ALSO** include **accurate and relevant information** from your **own knowledge** about why Scotsmen joined the army in 1914. You can get up to **7 marks** for this part of your answer.

As you write, ask yourself if the information you are including helps to answer the question to reach a balanced answer – or are you just including stuff you know without really thinking about whether it answers the question?

What is recall?

Recall means the detailed, factual information you know about a certain topic. When evaluating a source, recall can mean using your knowledge to explain more fully a point already made in the source. It does not always have to be a completely new point.

Question Type 4 is a 'How fully…' Question and is worth 10 Marks.

This question is to test your knowledge of a whole issue. Remember there are four issues in the syllabus that can be examined.

It could ask 'How fully does Source A illustrate the impact of the war on Scottish industry and the economy?' Most of the words in this question come straight from Issue 3 in the syllabus.

Just as in the other 10 mark question, you can get up to **4 marks** for **explaining** the points in the source **relevant to the question**. You can then get up to **7 marks** for relevant **detailed recall** that helps answer the question directly.

Now do some training!

Read this before you start answering questions. It will help you to improve your answers.

Activities

1   After each worked example you will see another question for you to try yourself. Read again the advice about writing a good answer.

2   Write your answer.

3   Exchange your answer with a partner. Use the information you already have about how marks are given to judge the value of your partner's answer. Return the marked answer. If there is any disagreement or difficulty ask your teacher to referee!

4   Once you have agreed the final mark take time to think about why you got the mark you did. Make two columns. Title one column 'What I did well'. Title the other column 'What I could improve on'. Use the feedback from your partner, your teacher and your own thoughts about your mark to complete the columns. Next time you do this type of question remember these columns!

The reason for doing this exercise is to understand and use the mark scheme. Once you know how marks are given you can structure your own answers to provide what markers are looking for.

Question Type 1 – Source Evaluation

Here is an example of a source evaluation question.

Source A is from a letter written by Private Douglas Hepburn of the London Scottish to his parents in October 1915.

Source A

My dear mum and dad,

We have been in the trenches for ten days and had a very rough time of it coming out with only 160 men left in our battalion. The Germans at the point where we attacked were ready and too strong for us. As we rushed up to the edge the machine gun was turned on us and we suffered high casualties. In the morning we came back and the sight of the field was rotten. It was a typical battlefield – see all the dead bodies lying about in different positions, all our own men of course, especially just in front of the German's barbed wire. To see thousands of our troops, stretching right across the plain to the horizon, and stretcher-bearers going here and there, doing their work and the wounded crying for the bearers. It was a sight that could not easily be forgotten on that grey, misty and damp morning.

How useful is Source A as evidence of the experience of Scottish soldiers on the Western Front? **(5 marks)**

Here is a weak answer:

The source is useful because it gives a description of a trench battle. It says they have lost a lot of men – 'coming out with only 160 men in our battalion'. It shows how the Germans were strong and defended behind barbed wire – 'The Germans at the point where we attacked were ready and too strong for us' and 'in front of the German's barbed wire'. The source is useful because it shows that soldiers were upset by all the deaths – 'It was a sight that could not easily be forgotten'.

Why is this a weak answer?

This answer is weak mainly because:

(1) The answer fails to evaluate by referring to the origins and possible purpose of the source.

(2) The answer just describes the source.

(3) The answer is useful in the detail it gives about what happened to Douglas Hepburn, but mainly it just copies phrases of the source.

(4) The answer contains no recalled knowledge.

(5) There is no attempt to provide a balanced answer suggesting the source might have its limits as a useful piece of evidence.

Marks

● There is no attempt to deal with origin or purpose (0 marks).

● It selects some relevant information from the source. However, it just lists some relevant points from the source. It does not explain why the evidence selected is relevant to the question (1 mark).

● There is no recall (0 marks).

Total achieved: 1 mark out of 5.

Here is a much better answer:

This source is partly useful for finding out about the experience of Scottish soldiers on the Western Front but it has limits.

The source is from a soldier on the Western Front so he is an eyewitness who experienced what he describes. The purpose is to let his parents

*know how he is getting on and what his experiences are like. This
makes the source very useful as primary evidence giving first hand
detail. As it is a letter to his parents the writer is likely to tell the truth
but maybe not details that would worry his parents. Letters were often
censored but this one seems to have got past the censor.*

*The detail given matches up with what I know. In trench warfare the
defence was usually stronger than the attackers and barbed wire and
machine guns usually caused the high casualties mentioned in the
source. The source mentions the stronger German position and that
was also usually true. The Germans chose to dig trenches on slightly
higher ground where they could see an attack coming.*

*The source does, however, have limits. It gives no information about
trench life such as the lice, the food, the boredom or the fear. There is
also information missing about battles such as heavy artillery barrages
and even gas.*

*Overall the source is quite useful for giving an impression but many
more letters would be needed to gain a full picture of the experience of
Scottish soldiers on the Western Front.*

Why is this a much better answer?

It is a better answer because:

(1) It not only identifies the origin and purpose of the source but
explains why each makes it a useful source (2 marks).

(2) It provides detail of trench warfare that matches other reports and
does make clear how the evidence selected is relevant to the question
(2 marks).

(3) It includes detailed recalled information. It also provides a balanced
evaluation of the usefulness of the source and includes more recall
that helps evaluate the evidence in terms of the question asked
(2 marks).

Marks

This answer scores highly simply by following the three stage marking
scheme process. The maximum number of marks for a Type 1 question
is 5 so even if this answer dropped a mark on a section, the writer would
still gain full marks.

Now try it yourself

Source B is adapted from an explanation by Robert Irvine of why he joined the army in 1914 in *Voices from War: Personal Recollections of War in our Century by Scottish Men and Women* (MacDougall, 1995).

Source B

When Lord Kitchener's pointing finger was on every hoarding throughout the country – 'Your King and Country Needs You' – I was one of the innocents who joined-up in this wave of patriotism at the beginning of the First World War.

I was only a shop assistant at the time, and on reflection I think it was more that I wanted to escape from the humdrum life behind a grocer's counter and see a bit of the country. I've since been sorry that I took that decision but I was just caught in the excitement of the times.

How useful is Source B in explaining the reasons why so many Scots volunteered for the British Army in 1914? (5 marks)

You should refer to:

- *the origin and possible purpose of the source*
- *the content of the source*
- *recalled knowledge.*

Question Type 2 – The Comparison Question

Source A is from Charlie Davies, a Scot who lived in London during the war. In 1975 he was interviewed about his experiences of the First World War.

Source A

When I came back after the war my family told me how bad it had been. You see, us being an island hardly any food could get through, because German U-boats were sinking our food convoys. My family lived on bones from the butcher made into soups. And stale bread. When some food did get delivered to the shops everyone for miles around crowded round the place. The queues stretched for miles, and if you were old or unsteady on your feet you stood no chance. Many, especially children, died of starvation. Food riots were very common.

Source B is from the *War Memoirs* of David Lloyd George (1938).

Source B

So far as the vast bulk of the population was concerned, this rationing system ensured a regular and sufficient food supply; and it made it possible for those in charge to calculate with some precision how best they could make the stocks of available foodstuffs go round fairly. Although there was a degree of scarcity, we were never faced with famine or actual privation. The steady improvement in our national health figures during and after the war shows that compulsory temperance in eating was in general more beneficial than harmful in its effects. Credit is due to our people for the loyal manner in which they submitted themselves to these strange and unwelcome restrictions. Without general goodwill it would have been impossible to make the regulations effective.

> To what extent do Sources A and B agree about the supply of food during the Great War? **(5 marks)**
>
> *You should compare the content overall and in detail.*

Here is a weak answer:

> *The two sources are about food supply in the war.*
>
> *One thinks the supply was bad. It says, 'Food riots were very common'. The other thinks it is good. It says, 'this rationing system ensured a regular and sufficient food supply'.*
>
> *One said, 'Many, especially children, died of starvation' and the other ones says, 'Credit is due to our people for the loyal manner in which they submitted themselves to these strange and unwelcome restrictions.'*
>
> *The sources are both about food supply but they say different things.*

Why is this a weak answer?

(1) There is no attempt to introduce the answer with an overall comparison.

(2) The writer does not identify what sources are being used at any time.

(3) The writer simply writes extracts from the sources and barely explains the point or meaning.

(4) Two extracts written from the sources are not about the same things so a direct comparison cannot be made.

Marks

There are only two points that **MIGHT** be considered as comparisons.

At **MOST** this answer would get 2 marks out of 5.

Here is a much better answer:

Overall the sources are about food supply during the war. Source A believes food shortages caused big problems whereas Source B claims the food supplies were controlled and organised so everyone had enough to eat.

In detail Charlie Davies reports that hardly any food could get through whereas Lloyd George states there was a regular and sufficient food supply.

Davies refers to the U Boat campaign which became more serious in 1917 when unrestricted submarine warfare began and all ships to Britain were targets. At that time the government introduced food rationing.

Davies claims the food shortages led to serious problems – 'Many, especially children, died of starvation' – while Lloyd George states, 'we were never faced with famine or actual privation'. It's possible that Davies is exaggerating as he only heard those stories when he came back from the war. On the other hand Lloyd George was Prime Minister so he would make the system sound as if it all worked well.

Davies claims his family only lived on 'bones from the butcher made into soups. And stale bread'. Lloyd George states 'compulsory temperance in eating was in general more beneficial than harmful in its effects'. Rationing was an attempt to make sure people got fair shares. As food supplies became scarcer prices started to rise. Food rationing stopped some people having too much food but made sure everyone had enough.

Davies also says that 'When some food did get delivered to the shops everyone for miles around crowded round the place.' Photographs of the time do show long queues. Lloyd George says, 'the rationing system ensured a regular food supply'. That was also true. Some rationed food was scarcer so people had to queue when supplies did eventually arrive.

Finally Davies claims 'Food riots were very common' whereas Lloyd George says, 'Without general goodwill it would have been impossible to make the regulations effective.' Overall food rationing made sure everyone got a fair share of food rather than using the black market and paying high prices.

Both sources may not be entirely accurate. Charlie Davies was reporting stories he had been told which might be exaggerated. Lloyd George is writing his memoirs which are always meant to make the politician look good so naturally rationing is described as a success.

Why is this a good answer?

(1) The answer starts with an overall comparison that shows understanding of both sources (2 marks).

(2) The answer then gives at least four direct comparisons.

(3) The comparisons are relevant and connected to each other.

(4) The comparisons are identified by the author's name.

(5) Recall is used to explain attitudes or details mentioned in the extracts.

(6) The answer contains comparisons of opinion but provides reasons for the differences.

Marks

This answer gains 5 marks out of 5. This answer scores highly because it follows the marking scheme process.

Now try it yourself

Source C is from *Memory Hold the Door* by John Buchan, published in 1940.

Source C

Haig had difficulties with his allies, with his colleagues, with the Government. At first he clung to traditional methods. He did not revise his plans until the old ones had been fully tested. A smaller man might have tried fantastic experiments that would have assuredly spelt disaster. Under him we incurred heavy losses, but I believe that these losses would have been greater if we had been led by someone less steady. Haig cannot enter the small circle of great leaders, but it may be argued that in the special circumstances of the war his special qualities were the ones most needed – patience, calmness and unshakeable determination.

Source D is from Charles Hudson, quoted in *Soldier, Poet, Rebel* (2007).

Source D

It is difficult to see how Haig, as Commander-in-Chief living in the atmosphere he did, so cut off from the fighting troops, could fulfill the tremendous task that was laid upon him effectively. I did not believe then, and I do not believe now that the enormous casualties were justified. Throughout the war huge bombardments failed again and again yet we persisted in employing the same hopeless method of attack. Many other methods were possible.

To what extent does Source C agree with Source D about the leadership of Sir Douglas Haig? **(5 marks)**

You should compare the content overall and in detail.

Question Type 3 – the 'How far...' Question

This is the question that asks about a specific part of an issue and wants to find out how much you know on the subject. A useful way to start an answer to this type of question is to say '**partly**'. That gives a basic answer to the question, 'How far...'

The source will provide relevant information but will not give the whole picture. That allows you to include other information relevant to the answer from your own knowledge in order to provide a full answer.

There are two phases to any answer to this type of question:

(1) You must select relevant points from the source and develop each point with recalled detailed knowledge. There are four marks available for doing this.

(2) You must then bring in your own knowledge to show there are other points relevant to the answer that are not in the sources. This part is worth up to 7 marks.

Here is an example of a 'how far' question:

Source A is from *Scottish Journey* by Edwin Muir, published in 1935.

Source A

By 1933 the Clyde was launching merely 56,000 tons of shipping, and the coal industry was finding work for only 80,000 hands and producing a third less coal than in 1913. The Dundee jute trade was deeply depressed and the Borders woollen industry for the greater part of the year was on part-time working. The output of Scottish farming was falling while it was still rising in England, and in the fishing industry the numbers of those employed and the value of the catch were both steadily dropping.

How far does Source A give evidence of post-war economic change and difficulties facing the Scottish economy? **(10 marks)**

Use the source and recalled knowledge.

Here is a weak answer:

The source gives quite good evidence of post-war economic change and difficulty. It says, 'the Clyde was launching merely 56,000 tons of shipping' which shows the shipbuilding industry was in decline.

The source says, 'the coal industry was finding work for only 80,000 hands and producing a third less coal than in 1913'. This means less coal was produced.

It says, 'the woollen industry for the greater part of the year was on part-time working'. That means people were not earning a full week's wage.

It says, 'The output of Scottish farming was falling' but then says English farms were doing better.

It also says the fishing industry was in difficulties so less people were employed.

Why is this a weak answer?

This answer is weak mainly because:

(1) The answer relies almost entirely on the information provided in the source.

(2) There is very little detailed recalled knowledge used to develop the points.

(3) There is no mention of any other areas of the economy facing change or difficulties which is necessary in this sort of evaluation question. In other words the candidate ignores the 'How far' part of the question.

Marks

The candidate only uses the source and makes the most limited development points so it will only gain a maximum of 2 out of 4 marks.

There is no recall in terms of the question to provide any balance so this candidate gets 0 marks out of 7 for this part.

Total 2 marks out of 10.

Here is a much better answer:

The source partly gives good evidence of post-war economic change and difficulty. It says, 'the Clyde was launching merely 56,000 tons of shipping'. The use of merely suggests it was in decline and before the war Clyde shipbuilding was booming. After the war international trade declined and so did demand for ships. The war had artificially boosted the industry but as orders dried up production fell.

The source mentions falling numbers of workers in the coal industry. As seams became less profitable more mines closed. New fuels, foreign competition and the lack of investment by owners made the coal industry decline.

Scottish farming also faced difficulties compared with England and that had much to do with climate and geography. New technology benefited larger farms but in Scotland the lack of good arable land made farming difficult.

The Scottish fishing industry was hit by war and revolution. Much of Scotland's herring catch was exported to Germany and Russia but during the war those markets were lost. The Russian revolution closed off exports to central Europe after the war. Fishing boats had been taken over by the navy and were in need of repair and replacement.

The jute industry also faced foreign competition and loss of export markets. New factories near Calcutta and also the Far East took away Dundee's trade.

Other parts of the economy also suffered. Mainly Scotland's staple industries were all interlinked. Iron and steel used coal and depended on demand from shipbuilding for the iron and steel. As shipbuilding declined with world trade so did the other connected industries. These are examples but not the difficulties – unemployment, falling trade, continued decline of staples.

Talent in Scotland also left through emigration, sometimes to England or abroad.

In the Highlands the land question meant that farms remained relatively unproductive and inefficient.

Overall the source gives a good impression of an economy in decline but not the reasons for it, nor does it give the whole picture.

Why is this a much better answer?

It is a better answer because:

(1) It selects information from the source and uses recalled knowledge to develop each point.

(2) It provides a balance to the answer by using a lot of recall about other industries and other parts of the economy.

(3) It ends with a short conclusion that shows the candidate has understood the question and thought about its meaning.

Marks

This answer scores highly simply by following the marking scheme process.

The candidate uses the source and develops the points well so gains 4 marks out of 4.

There is a lot of recall and most of it is relevant. Sometimes the explanations are weak, such as with farming and the Highlands, but overall this part of the answer should get at least 5 marks out of 7, giving a total of 9 marks out of 10.

Now try it yourself

Source B is a speech by James Maxton, a socialist who objected to conscription, at his tribunal.

Source B

I am a socialist and a member of a socialist organisation. As such I have worked to establish a better system of society, which would make for the peace and brotherhood of peoples of all lands. To take part in a war would be for me a desertion of these ideals, and I must therefore decline to take part.

How far does Source B represent the ideas of conscientious objectors?
(10 marks)

Use the source and recalled knowledge.

Question Type 4 – The 'How fully...' Question

This is the question that asks about a specific issue within the syllabus and wants to find out how much you know on the subject. A useful way to start an answer to this type of question is to say '**partly**'. That gives a basic answer to the question, 'How fully...'

The source will provide relevant information, but will not give the whole picture. That allows you to include other information relevant to the answer from your own knowledge in order to provide a full answer.

There are two phases to any answer to this type of question:

(1) You must select relevant points from the source and develop each point with recalled detailed knowledge. There are 4 marks available for doing this.

(2) You must then bring in your own knowledge to show there are other points relevant to the answer that are not in the sources. This part is worth up to 7 marks.

Here is an example of a 'How fully...' question:

Source A is from a speech by David Kirkwood against the Munitions Act, made at Glasgow City Hall in 1916.

Source A

Fellow engineers, the country is at war. The country must win. In order to win, we must throw our whole soul into the production of munitions. Now we come to the point of difference. The Government and its supporters think that to get the best out of us, they must take away our liberty. So we are deprived of the chief thing that distinguishes free men from slaves, the right to leave a master when we wish to. If I work in Beardmore's I am as much his property as if he had branded a 'B' on my brow.

Mr Lloyd George claims that all this is necessary in order to win the War. I deny it. We are willing, as we have always been, to do our bit, but we object to slavery.

> How fully does Source A explain the
> Scottish impact of the war on political
> society? **(10 marks)**
>
> *Use the source and recalled knowledge.*

Here is a weak answer to the question:

> *The Munitions Act put workers under military control and Kirkwood
> does not like that. During the war the government had to make sure
> they had enough munitions produced so they tried to make sure that
> workers could not go on strike or disrupt production. Kirkwood
> agrees Britain needed to win the war but he objected to increasing
> government control. During the war the government increased its
> control over most people's lives with changes such as rationing
> and conscription.*

Why is this a weak answer?

The answer understands Kirkwood's point about government control
but should have explained more fully the restrictions the government
placed on workers' freedom to move jobs. It makes no attempt to look at
the wider issue of political changes in Scotland. The main weakness in
this answer is that the candidate does not move away from the source.
There should be a wider answer dealing with the impact of the war on
politics in Scotland.

Marks

The candidate only really makes the point about increasing government
control and that some workers resented it.

This part can only get a maximum of 2 marks out of 4. There is only
one piece of recall that **MIGHT** gain a mark. In total, this answer
would get no more than 3 marks out of 10.

Here is a much better answer:

> *The Munitions Act put workers under military control and Kirkwood
> does not like that. During the war the government had to make sure
> they had enough munitions produced so they tried to make sure that
> workers could not go on strike or disrupt production. Kirkwood
> agrees Britain needed to win the war but he objected to increasing
> government control. During the war the government increased its
> control over most people's lives with changes such as rationing and
> conscription.*

This was one of the complaints that led to worker protests that became known as Red Clydeside. During the war some workers became supporters of socialism and the Independent Labour Party. Elsewhere the middle classes turned to the Conservative or Unionist party to save them from possible revolution. Scotland became divided between left-wing supporters and right-wing supporters and the old-fashioned Liberal Party broke in two and never had power again. The overall impact of the war was that it changed Scottish politics.

Why is this a better answer?

This is a better answer but is still not perfect. The answer at least brings in relevant recall and shows an understanding of the changes in Scottish politics brought about by the war. The whole issue cannot be covered in this answer but equally it must be understood that this question needs an overview of the main points in the issue to be successful.

Marks

This answer would still only gain 2 marks out of 4 for developing the source but could gain 4 marks out of 7 for relevant recall, making a total of 6 marks out of 10.

Now try it yourself

Source B is by John A. Kerr from *Scotland and the Impact of the Great War 1914–1928*.

Source B

In 1914 the UK had a Liberal government and in Scotland the Liberals were the most powerful political party. The Conservative and Unionist Party was much less important and represented mainly rural areas and especially the wealthy land-owning class. The Labour Party had not yet made any significant breakthrough into national politics.

By 1918 the landscape of British and Scottish politics had changed completely. The Liberal Party had split and after the mid-1920s they would never again be a significant force in British politics. The Conservative and Unionist Party recovered from its poor pre-war election results and began to attract new voters from the middle classes in the cities. The Independent Labour Party was stronger in 1918 than it had been in 1914 and the mainstream Labour Party was about to become one of the two big parties in British politics.

How fully does Source B illustrate the
impact of the war on political developments
in Scotland? **(10 marks)**

References

Chapter 1

Devine, T.M. (2004) *Scotland's Empire 1600–1815*, London: Penguin

Devine, T.M. (2006) *The Scottish Nation: 1700–2007*, London: Penguin

Johnston, T. (1999) *Ours Scots Noble Families*, Argyll: Argyll Publishing

Marr, A. (1992) *The Battle for Scotland*, London: Penguin

Muir, E. (1996) *Scottish Journey*, Edinburgh: Mainstream Publishing

Royle, T. (2006) *The Flowers of the Forest: Scotland and the Great War*, Edinburgh: Birlinn Ltd

'What the Hebrides has done', *Inverness Courier*, 12 March 1915

Chapter 2

Buchan, J. (2008) *Mr. Standfast*, Hertfordshire: Wordsworth Classics

Gibbon, L.G. (1996) *Sunset Song*, Edinburgh: Canongate Classics

Macdonald, C.M.M. and McFarland, E.W. (1998) *Scotland and the Great War*, Edinburgh: Tuckwell Press

Royle, T. (2006) *The Flowers of the Forest: Scotland and the Great War*, Edinburgh: Birlinn Ltd

Young, D. (2005) *Scottish Voices from the Great War*, Stroud: Tempus Publishing

Times, Monday 9 August 2008 (letter)

Extracts from the diary of George Ramage, National Library of Scotland, MSS.944- 947

http://www.webmatters.net/france/ww1_loos_2.htm

http://www.spartacus.schoolnet.co.uk/FWWsomme.htm

http://www.spartacus.schoolnet.co.uk/FWWhaig.htm

Chapter 3

Macdonald, C.M.M. and McFarland, E.W. (1998) *Scotland and the Great War*, Edinburgh: Tuckwell Press

Royle, T. (2006) *The Flowers of the Forest: Scotland and the Great War*, Edinburgh: Birlinn Ltd

Extracts from *The Chisholm Papers*, Edinburgh: The National Library of Scotland

http://www.spartacus.schoolnet.co.uk/TUrussell.htm

http://www.spartacus.schoolnet.co.uk/FWWpacifists.htm

http://www.nationalarchives.gov.uk/pathways/firstworldwar/transcripts/first_world_war/defence_ofthe-realm.htm

Chapter 4

Devine, T.M. (2006) *The Scottish Nation: 1700–2007*, London: Penguin

Gibbon, L.G. (1996) *Sunset Song*, Edinburgh: Canongate Classics

Macdonald, C.M.M. and McFarland, E.W. (1998) *Scotland and the Great War*, Edinburgh: Tuckwell Press

McIver, D. (1906) *An Old Time Fishing Town: Eyemouth*, Greenock: James McKelvie and Son

Muir, E. (1996) *Scottish Journey*, Edinburgh: Mainstream Publishing

Royle, T. (2006) *The Flowers of the Forest: Scotland and the Great War*, Edinburgh: Birlinn Ltd

http://www.spartacus.schoolnet.co.uk/FWWrationing.htm

Chapter 5

Devine, T.M. (2006) *The Scottish Nation: 1700–2007*, London: Penguin

Gibbon, L.G. (1996) *Sunset Song*, Edinburgh: Canongate Classics

Macdonald, C.M.M. and McFarland, E.W. (1998) *Scotland and the Great War*, Edinburgh: Tuckwell Press

Royle, T. (2006) *The Flowers of the Forest: Scotland and the Great War*, Edinburgh: Birlinn Ltd

http://www.spartacus.schoolnet.co.uk/PRasquith.htm

http://www.spartacus.schoolnet.co.uk/TUkirkwoodD.htm

Chapter 6

Gibbon, L.G. (1996) *Sunset Song*, Edinburgh: Canongate Classics

Muir, E. (1996) *Scottish Journey*, Edinburgh: Mainstream Publishing

Preparing for Paper 2 of the Higher History Exam

Buchan, J. (1940) *Memory Hold the Door*, London: Hodder & Stoughton

Hudson, M. (2007) *Soldier, Poet, Rebel: The Extraordinary Life of Charles Hudson VC*, Stroud: The History Press

Lloyd George, D. *War Memoirs* (1938) Quoted on www.spartacus.schoolnet.co.uk/FWWrationing.htm

MacDougall, I. (1995) *Voices from War: Personal Recollections of War in our Century by Scottish Men and Women*, Edinburgh: Mercat Press

Muir, E. (1996) *Scottish Journey*, Edinburgh: Mainstream Publishing

Index